DARE TO DREAM

'The best moment of my life' - that's how Niall McGinn described his goal at Euro 2016.

UKRAINE VS NORTHERN IRELAND
16 JUNE 2016
STADE DE LYON

DARE TO DREAM

NORTHERN IRELAND'S EURO 2016 ADVENTURE

PICTURES: WILLIAM CHERRY

WORDS: MARK McINTOSH AND NIGEL TILSON

THE BLACK STAFF PRESS

Belfast
in association with
The Irish Football Assciation

First published in 2016 by
Blackstaff Press
4D Weavers Court
Linfield Road
Belfast
BT12 5GH

in association with

Irish Football Association
National Football Stadium at Windsor Park
Donegall Avenue
Belfast
BT12 6LW

Designed by seagulls.net

Printed in Italy by Printer Trento

A CIP catalogue record for this book is
available from the British Library

ISBN 978-0-85640-994-3

www.blackstaffpress.com
www.irishfa.com

CONTENTS

FOREWORD

From qualification to participation at the finals, the Euro 2016 adventure for Northern Ireland was something to savour. These are the moments you cherish in football.

Coming from behind to win against Hungary away in the first game of the qualifying campaign set us nicely on our way. It is, after all, always important to get a campaign off to a decent start. We gathered further momentum with a good win against the Faroes – our first home game in over a year due to the redevelopment work at the stadium – followed by that crucial night in Athens when we defeated Greece. The belief was really beginning to grow in the squad at that stage.

After losing in Romania, it was important to get the winning feeling back and we did that thanks to a fine victory over the Finns at home. We secured another point in the scoreless draw against Romania in Belfast and next stop was Torshavn and the Faroe Islands where patience and confidence within the team were evident.

Going into the Hungary game in Belfast we knew that three points would be enough to see Northern Ireland qualify for a major tournament for the first time in 30 years.

It was a real emotional rollercoaster of a game. The belief within the team again shone through when we fell behind only to grab a deserved point thanks to Kyle Lafferty's last-minute goal. Of course, it meant qualification was still just out of our grasp. However, we also knew a win at home against Greece would take us to France.

The players who entered the fray against the Greeks in place of those who were either suspended or missing through injury showed me once again that our squad has the hunger, passion and desire to tackle any challenge. It was a night when new heroes emerged and the job got done thanks to a terrific team performance. The feeling of elation at the final whistle is something I will never forget.

We were still on a high when we faced the Finns in our final group game a few days later and it was great to come away with the point that put us top of the group.

After the finals draw at the Palais des Congrès in Paris last December our preparations for Euro 2016 really gathered pace as we knew which teams we would be facing in France and where we would be playing our group games.

We settled on a hotel north of Lyon for our base camp, and a pitch at a nearby small sports complex as our training ground, and both turned out to be ideal.

Our warm-up games and training camps prior to arriving in France all went well and we prepared meticulously for our opening game.

It was a huge occasion in Nice, especially given the fact it was Northern Ireland's first ever game at a European Championship finals. Of course, it did not go according to plan, and we were disappointed at losing to Poland in front of so many of our fans. However, that game was quickly forgotten when we played Ukraine. The players were determined to bounce back and they did so with a huge performance to give us a chance of qualifying for the knockout stages. And the atmosphere created by our fans in Lyon was simply electric.

The match against Germany in Paris saw us produce another huge performance. We knew that we might need a point and that goal difference could be a deciding factor. The Germans were mesmerising but thanks to a fantastic performance by Michael McGovern, and a gritty display from the team, we secured a result that would ultimately help us qualify for the Round of 16 – and that was an incredible achievement.

It was then a case of waiting to see whom we would face next. Robbie Brady's 85th-minute winner for the Republic of Ireland against Italy meant we would not be playing France in Lyon, as we had hoped, but instead would be back in Paris to face Wales.

There was a lot of tension in the game against the Welsh but we produced another great performance. We were the better team and created some decent chances but it was not to be. And Gareth's own goal was a cruel way to lose the game.

Naturally, we were all dejected going home. However, we took great pride in our performances. It was a wrench to leave France, especially when we felt our stay should have been longer, but returning to Belfast and seeing the effect our performances had had on the whole country made us all immensely proud. The homecoming event at Titanic Belfast was a fitting finale to an incredible adventure.

Michael O'Neill
Northern Ireland Manager

Niall McGinn is mobbed by his team-mates after scoring against Ukraine in France. Stuart Dallas (left) and Josh Magennis (right) played key roles in the lead-up to the goal.

WHEN THE DREAM BECAME A REALITY ...

Thursday 8 October 2015 was the date when everything we had dared to dream became a reality.

In front of a half-built but fully packed National Football Stadium at Windsor Park the modern Greeks were put to the sword by Steven Davis and his team, and as the final whistle blew it was time to start booking tickets for France. Yes, after a gap of 30 years, Northern Ireland and the GAWA were on their way to taking a place at a major tournament.

The next few months passed in a blur of planning and anticipation, the highlight of which was a trip to Paris in December 2015 to learn that we had been grouped with Poland, Ukraine and the world champions Germany.

But we weren't worried – we knew that we weren't there just to make up the numbers. And Michael had a plan. The fans quickly got themselves onto Google Maps to work out the distances between Nice, Lyon and Paris and snapped up thousands of tickets as soon as they became available.

After a raucous send-off party at the National Football Stadium on 27 May 2016 – where Belarus played their part well in a 3-0 Northern Ireland victory – the squad made their final preparations in Austria, before a last tune-up game against Slovakia in Trnava and then on to the base camp near Lyon.

Sunday 12 June – 30 years to the day since we had last played in a major tournament – came quickly and the Stade de Nice was the stage for our first match of the tournament. Although Poland took the points from this game, the atmosphere and noise from the GAWA was incredible and more than a few people admitted to being emotional that day.

The match against Ukraine at the Stade de Lyon was next up. The team played through a hailstorm this time but the 'Kings of Lyon' outclassed the men in yellow to put us back in contention with two unforgettable goals from Gareth McAuley and Niall McGinn.

And so to Paris. If someone had said on 7 September 2014 that our Euro adventure would at least take us to Paris to play the world champions on 21 June 2016 we would have taken that without question. Germany played extremely well and took a first-half lead but Michael McGovern repelled everything else they could throw at him – and with results later that evening going our way we were in the last 16!

Nearly an hour after the final whistle in Paris, the GAWA were still in the stadium and celebrating in full voice. Germany star Bastian Schweinsteiger became an early admirer of the incredible feel-good atmosphere our fans generated, and was later joined by the Mayor of Paris and the President of UEFA in a chorus of approval for our incredible supporters.

Northern Ireland's story ended four days later, back in Paris, when we lost to the Welsh, many of whom admitted we had been the better team on the day. That's the essence of sport though, winners and losers – we all know the drill.

We might have lost in the Round of 16 but in a bigger sense we were, and still are, winners. Our squad, our backroom staff, our coaches, our administrators and our supporters were the best of a new Northern Ireland. Major tournaments are all the poorer when we are not around to light them up. I can't wait to do it all again.

Patrick Nelson
Chief Executive
Irish Football Association

Michael O'Neill is raised high by the players and the fans jump for joy as Northern Ireland qualify for the Euros.

CHAPTER ONE
THE ROAD TO FRANCE

HUNGARY 1 - 2 NORTHERN IRELAND

Niall McGinn celebrates his goal.

7 September 2014

Groupama Arena, Budapest

Attendance: 20,672

This was the game that changed everything when Northern Ireland's campaign in the UEFA European Championship Qualifying Group F got under way. After a solid defensive display, Michael O'Neill's men were one goal down 15 minutes from time. Defender Gareth McAuley had gone off injured and had been replaced by Craig Cathcart. However, it was another substitution that turned the game on its head. Niall McGinn replaced Jamie Ward on 66 minutes and with nine minutes left on the clock the Aberdeen ace levelled the scores, thanks to an assist from Kyle Lafferty, who broke into the penalty area and squared the ball across goal for McGinn to tap home unchallenged. There was even better to come as the double act struck again. This time it was McGinn who did the hard work before crossing for Lafferty who managed to nudge the ball over the line from close range with two minutes remaining. It was the perfect start for Northern Ireland in the campaign, as well as being their first away win in 18 matches. Michael O'Neill wanted momentum and his squad came up trumps. This game also saw Chris Brunt impress at left back, a position he was to make his own throughout the qualifying campaign. As for Hungary boss Attila Pintér, the match marked the end of the road for him and he lost his job.

Ollie Norwood goes for a tumble during the game.

Kyle Lafferty is loving life after scoring the winner.

LINE-UP: Carroll, McLaughlin, McAuley (Cathcart 72'), Hughes, Brunt, Baird, Corry Evans, Norwood (McKay 79'), Davis, Ward (McGinn 66'), Kyle Lafferty.

SUBS: Daniel Lafferty, Cathcart, McGinn, McKay, Mannus, McCullough, Grigg, Ferguson, Little, Magennis, Paton, McGovern.

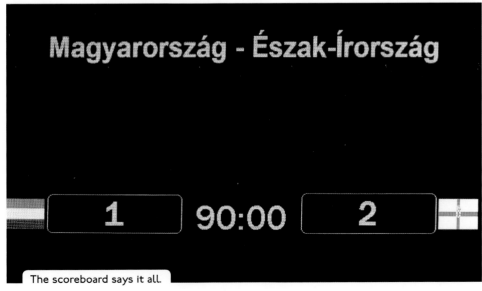

Magyarország - Észak-Írország

| 1 | 90:00 | 2 |

The scoreboard says it all.

NORTHERN IRELAND 2 - 0 FAROE ISLANDS

11 October 2014

National Football Stadium at
Windsor Park

Attendance: 10,049

Having earned the comeback victory in Budapest, Northern Ireland were under pressure to take full advantage against the Faroe Islands, who were seen as the weakest team in Group F. And there was to be no banana skin this time as Northern Ireland raced out of the blocks in a slightly different-looking Windsor Park. Redevelopment work had begun and only two sides of the stadium were in use but the noise was as loud as ever when Gareth McAuley calmly slotted home Chris Baird's knockdown after only six minutes. Then Kyle Lafferty made it two goals in two games when he scored on 20 minutes, flicking Shane Ferguson's pinpoint cross beyond the Faroes' keeper Gunnar

Neilsen. There was a worrying moment 10 minutes before the half-time break, however, when the visitors were awarded a penalty after Ferguson brought down Jóan Símun Edmundsson, but Roy Carroll dived low to his left to push Fróði Benjaminsen's spot-kick onto the post. Neilsen denied Ollie Norwood a first international goal when he palmed a second-half piledriver onto the crossbar but three points were already in the bag thanks to the early strikes. This was already Northern Ireland's best start to any qualifying campaign since 1968.

LINE-UP: Carroll, Conor McLaughlin, McAuley (McCullough 56'), Hughes, Ferguson, Baird, Ward, Davis, Norwood, McGinn (McCourt 67'), Lafferty (Magennis 84').

SUBS: McGivern, McCullough, McKay, Mannus, Corry Evans, Clingan, McCourt, Ryan McLaughlin, Magennis, Reeves, McGovern.

Goalkeeper Roy Carroll applauds the fans.

Gareth McAuley celebrates his goal.

Kyle Lafferty tussles with Faroese defenders.

Conor McLaughlin makes a clearance.

GREECE 0 - 2 NORTHERN IRELAND

The defeat against Northern Ireland led to Greece's manager Claudio Ranieri losing his job.

14 October 2014

Karaiskakis Stadium, Piraeus

Attendance: 18,726

With a 100 per cent record in the opening two games, Northern Ireland travelled to Athens believing they could get a positive result. But they didn't just beat Greece, they produced a heroic display against Claudio Ranieri's top seeds. Gareth McAuley, celebrating his 50th cap, chose not to take the captain's armband from Steven Davis as he didn't want to change what wasn't broken. And there was another quick-fire start as Jamie Ward's shot deflected off Loukas Vyntra to give Michael O'Neill's men the lead. But it was to get even better for the visitors on 51 minutes when Kyle Lafferty produced one of the best individual goals seen anywhere in Europe during the campaign. He raced from his own half after an incisive pass from Chris Baird and held off the home defence before firing low into the corner from the edge of the box. The celebrations on the pitch were as spectacular as they were in the stands. Northern Ireland had begun the campaign with three wins in a row - something they had never managed to achieve in their history - and were sitting at the top of the group after three games, two points clear of their closest opponents. Players and supporters alike were daring to dream of making it to France.

LINE-UP: Carroll, Conor McLaughlin, McAuley, Hughes, Ferguson (Reeves 78'), Baird, Corry Evans, Davis, Norwood, Ward (McGivern 59'), Lafferty (Magennis 73').

SUBS: McGivern, McCullough, McGinn, McKay, Mannus, Clingan, McCourt, Grigg, Ryan McLaughlin, Magennis, Reeves, McGovern.

Jamie Ward is in high spirits after his goal against the Greeks.

Gareth McAuley won his 50th cap in the game against Greece. Goals from Jamie Ward and Kyle Lafferty secured a 2-0 win in Piraeus.

ROMANIA 2 - 0 NORTHERN IRELAND

14 November 2014

Arena Naţională, Bucharest

Attendance: 28,892

Northern Ireland were dealt a major blow in the build-up to the Romania game when inspirational skipper Steven Davis was ruled out of the trip to Bucharest due to an injury. Jamie Ward was also absent with a knock, meaning that the attacking options were not as strong as they had been in the opening three games. Anghel Iordănescu was beginning his third spell as Romania coach and his side always looked the more likely to open the scoring. Chris Brunt threatened with a shot that flew just past the post but the home side were on top. Alexandru Chipciu shot against the underside of the bar and then headed straight at Roy Carroll. With Romania assuming control, playmaker Lucian Sânmărtaen picked up the ball on the halfway line and waltzed through the Northern Ireland defence only for Bogdan Stancu to lose his footing with the goal gaping. Kyle Lafferty, looking for his fourth strike in as many games, had a shot palmed away by Ciprian Tătăruşanu. After the break Carroll stood up well to deny Romania captain Răzvan Raţ but Northern Ireland's brave resistance came to an end 16 minutes from time – and the goal came from an unlikely source. Full-back Paul Papp rocketed a shot into the top corner after Michael O'Neill's men had failed to clear and he made it two in the space of six minutes when he stole in at the back post to condemn an under-strength Northern Ireland to their first – and ultimately only – defeat of the campaign.

Northern Ireland fans check out some of the sights in Bucharest prior to the game.

The Arena Naţională in Bucharest.

Ryan McGivern challenges for the ball.

Chris Brunt in the thick of the action in Bucharest.

Corry Evans in a midfield tussle.

LINE-UP: Carroll, McLaughlin, McAuley, Hughes, McGivern, Baird, McGinn (Clingan 63'), Corry Evans (McKay 79'), Norwood, Brunt, Lafferty.

SUBS: McCullough, Clingan, McKay, Mannus, McCourt, McNair, Grigg, Cathcart, Magennis, Reeves, McGovern.

NORTHERN IRELAND 2 – 1 FINLAND

29 March 2015

National Football Stadium at Windsor Park

Attendance: 10,264

Northern Ireland made it four wins from five as they celebrated their 600th competitive game. It was a unique occasion as the Northern Ireland team were playing a home international on a Sunday for the first time, though the day of the week was irrelevant for them – they just wanted another three points. This encounter saw Jonny Evans play his first game of the qualifying campaign. He had missed the opening four games due to injury, but given his undoubted class O'Neill had no hesitation in bringing him straight back into his starting line-up at the expense of the experienced Aaron Hughes. Chris Baird's header was ruled out for offside and Jamie Ward spurned a great chance but once again it was star striker Kyle Lafferty who produced moments of magic to seal the victory. At club level he left Norwich City on a loan move to Turkish side Çaykur Rizespor to make sure his fitness was as sharp as possible and he delivered the goods not once but twice in this match, continuing his already remarkable scoring run with a clinical finish after latching onto a header from Niall McGinn to volley into the net. He then doubled his side's lead when he headed Conor McLaughlin's terrific cross beyond keeper Lukas Hradecky. Berat Sadik grabbed a late consolation for the Finns after Roy Carroll palmed out Roman Eremenko's initial drive. And the goal stood even though television replays showed it was offside. Off the pitch there was more drama. Less than 48 hours after the final whistle some cracks were discovered in the West Stand. It was immediately closed and would later be demolished.

Stuart Dallas flies high during the home qualifier against Finland.

Kyle Lafferty makes his presence felt during the match against the Finns.

LINE-UP: Carroll, McLaughlin, McAuley, Jonny Evans, Brunt, Davis (Corry Evans 45'), Baird, Norwood, Ward, Kyle Lafferty (Magennis 79'), McGinn (Dallas 64').

SUBS: Daniel Lafferty, McKay, Mannus, Corry Evans, Dallas, McCourt, McNair, Hughes, McCullough, Magennis, Grigg, McGovern.

Jonny Evans jumps for joy at the final whistle.

NORTHERN IRELAND 0 – 0 ROMANIA

Northern Ireland and Romania take to the pitch in Belfast.

13 June 2015

National Football Stadium at Windsor Park

Attendance: 10,000

This game was always going to be tricky, and not just because Romania were now sitting at the top of Group F. Given the fact the qualifier was being played in June, long after the Northern Ireland players had finished their domestic season, it presented a few unfamiliar obstacles. But to a man Michael O'Neill's troops showed they had remained fully focused on the job in hand while club team-mates were enjoying family holidays. Goalkeeper Roy Carroll was forced to miss the game with an injury after starring in the opening five games. Goalkeeping coach Maik Taylor rolled back the years when he was named on the bench in case of an emergency as Michael McGovern was handed his first competitive start for his country. The game was not a memorable one as it presented very few chances. Kyle Lafferty had the best opportunity of the game. Gareth McAuley headed a free-kick down to the unmarked Lafferty but from eight yards the normally lethal hitman shot straight at a grateful Ciprian Tătăruşanu. It was a glorious chance and a rare miss from Lafferty. Ollie Norwood also saw a free-kick tipped over the bar and the top-of-the-table clash ended in stalemate.

LINE-UP: McGovern, McLaughlin, McAuley, Jonny Evans (Cathcart 80'), Brunt, Davis, Ward (Corry Evans 79'), Norwood, Baird, Dallas, Lafferty.

SUBS: Ferguson, McGinn, Grigg, Carson, Corry Evans, McCourt, McNair, Hughes, Cathcart, Magennis, Lavery, Taylor.

FAROE ISLANDS 1 – 3 NORTHERN IRELAND

4 September 2015

Tórsvøllur Stadium, Tórshavn

Attendance: 4,513

This was the kind of game that Northern Ireland had traditionally struggled in – but not this squad. Memories of the previous trip to the Faroes, which ended in a demoralising 1-1 draw, were well and truly banished with this performance. Michael O'Neill made a huge call in his starting line-up in sticking with keeper Michael McGovern despite Roy Carroll's return to full fitness. McGovern was used to playing on an artificial surface similar to the pitch in the Faroes. Gareth McAuley opened the scoring, just as he had done against the Faroese in Belfast, heading home on 12 minutes. But the home side levelled nine minutes before the interval thanks to a Jóan Símun Edmundsson strike. However, his joy turned to despair when he was sent off in the 64th minute,

giving O'Neill's men the boost they needed and marking a turning-point in the game. The 10-men home side were unable to cope with McAuley as he nodded his second goal of the game before Kyle Lafferty continued his terrific form with his sixth of the campaign. He showed great persistence to cement the hard-fought win in which set pieces proved vital. With Romania being held to a 0-0 draw in Hungary, Northern Ireland climbed back to the top of the table with just three games remaining. They were on the brink of qualifying for their first major tournament since the World Cup in Mexico in 1986 and victory over Hungary would be enough to do it.

LINE-UP: McGovern, McLaughlin (Magennis 69'), McAuley, Jonny Evans, Brunt (Ferguson 83'), Davis, Baird, McGinn, Norwood, Dallas, Lafferty (McNair 78').

SUBS: Ferguson, Grigg, Carroll, Corry Evans, McCourt, McNair, Hughes, McKay, Cathcart, Magennis, Boyce, Mannus.

Canon Edgar Turner, who sadly passed away earlier this year, was the oldest Northern Ireland fan at the away qualifier against the Faroe Islands. Then aged 95, Edgar was delighted to see his team triumph.

Gareth McAuley punches the air with delight after scoring.

Ollie Norwood tries a spot of ball juggling with a Faroese player.

NORTHERN IRELAND 1 – 1 HUNGARY

7 September 2015

National Football Stadium at Windsor Park

Attendance: 10,200

The objective was simple: to win. With that, qualification for Euro 2016 would be secured. The new-look National Football Stadium at Windsor Park was starting to take shape and was beginning to feel more like home. Northern Ireland were dominant throughout the first half but were unable to find the final ball or decisive touch in front of goal to open the scoring. Then came the sucker punch everyone had been dreading. Goalkeeper Michael McGovern made an uncharacteristic mistake when he failed to gather a straightforward free-kick from Balázs Dzsudzsák and gifted Richard Guzmics the opening goal 16 minutes from time. There were nervous faces all around the stadium and the situation became even more worrying on 81 minutes when Chris Baird was dismissed after receiving one of the most bizarre red cards ever seen at the famous stadium – new or old. Turkish referee Cüneyt Çakir caused confusion when he flashed two yellow cards, followed by a red, in the direction of Baird. Most people were expecting a yellow but the referee indicated he was cautioning Baird for two fouls in the same move after playing an advantage. Despite the fans praying for a late goal, O'Neill called for calm as a second goal for Hungary would have given them an advantage over Northern Ireland on the head-to-head rule. He needn't have worried, however. That double act of McGinn and Lafferty was in evidence again as super-sub McGinn's shot was palmed out and Lafferty converted it from close range. And Windsor Park erupted.

LINE-UP: McGovern, McLaughlin, McAuley, Jonny Evans, Brunt, Corry Evans (McGinn 56'), Davis, Baird, Norwood (Magennis 75'), Dallas (Ferguson 84'), Lafferty.

SUBS: Ferguson, McGinn, Grigg, Carroll, McCourt, McNair, Hughes, McKay, Cathcart, Magennis, Lavery, Mannus.

Jonny Evans in a tussle for possession.

Chris Brunt received his 50th cap from Irish FA President Jim Shaw before the game against Hungary.

Kyle Lafferty knocks in the late equaliser against Hungary.

Stuart Dallas gets to grips with the Hungarian midfield.

NORTHERN IRELAND 3 – 1 GREECE

8 October 2015

National Football Stadium at Windsor Park

Attendance: 11,700

Two points from the final two games would be enough for Northern Ireland to qualify. But Michael O'Neill was forced into making several changes as suspensions kicked in for the first time during the qualifying campaign. Conor McLaughlin, Chris Baird and talisman Kyle Lafferty were sitting in the stand along with Jonny Evans, who was ruled out with a hamstring injury. All of them were facing an agonising wait to see if their team-mates could produce the goods to get them over the line - and boy did they deliver. Captain Steven Davis scored twice and stand-in striker Josh Magennis bagged his first international goal. Davis, who was just one when his country last qualified for a major tournament, opened the scoring when he converted Stuart Dallas' low cross before the break. The Greeks threatened when Kostas Mitroglou hit the post on the stroke of half-time but once Magennis headed home after the break the outcome was never in doubt. Davis then headed a third from 16 yards as the party kicked off. Christos Aravidis scored a consolation but by that stage the Green and White Army were already booking flights to France. Hero Davis dedicated his double to his late mum and biggest fan, Laura, who passed away after a lengthy illness in 2008.

An iconic moment as Steven Davis looks heavenward as he celebrates one of his two goals against Greece. He is joined by Josh Magennis, who also scored in the famous 3-1 win.

Steven Davis wheels away in delight after scoring against the Greeks.

Michael McGovern punches clear during a rare attack by Greece.

Corry Evans outjumps a Greek player.

Josh Magennis in a battle for possession.

LINE-UP: McGovern, McNair (McCullough 85'), McAuley, Cathcart, Brunt, Davis, Ward (McGinn 81'), Corry Evans, Norwood, Dallas, Magennis (Boyce 78').

SUBS: Hodson, Ferguson, McCullough, Reeves, McGinn, Grigg, McKay, Carroll, McCourt, McArdle, Boyce, Mannus.

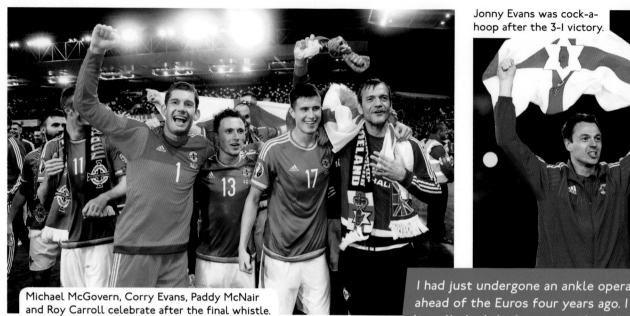

Jonny Evans was cock-a-hoop after the 3-1 victory.

Michael McGovern, Corry Evans, Paddy McNair and Roy Carroll celebrate after the final whistle.

I had just undergone an ankle operation ahead of the Euros four years ago. I literally had the leg propped up the whole tournament, sitting watching the games. Euro 2012 was a great tournament and I vividly remember thinking how fantastic it would be to play on such a stage with Northern Ireland. **JONNY EVANS**

Although the European Championship has gone up to 24 teams, no one can say we just got in because it opened up – we got in because we were good enough. We would have got in had it still only been 16 teams. It's an unbelievable achievement. **MICHAEL McGOVERN**

For 48 hours after the Greece game my face was everywhere. It was a whirlwind. I never expected any of it. The support and the love the fans give not just me but everyone in the squad is amazing. They've backed us no matter what and to do it for them and the nation was something we are all proud of. **JOSH MAGENNIS**

Josh Magennis was overjoyed after grabbing his goal.

The team and the squad enjoyed their lap of honour at Windsor Park after the match.

There was no talk about international football or France at my club, but the players back there have been really supportive. They've sent me messages saying good luck. We won the group and all that, but we'll come up against great teams. You see "Poland" in big letters in your head because it's the first game, and they have superstars, as do every team in France. **CONOR McLAUGHLIN**

I wouldn't say I'm a hero but the more I read and the more I heard I did enjoy going out and proving everybody wrong about me. There's great belief in the camp and we know we can pick up points. I think we're capable of frustrating teams and hitting them on the break. **KYLE LAFFERTY**

Our expectations as players are going up and naturally the fans' expectations have also been raised during the campaign. I think that just goes to show the massive strides we have made over the past couple of years. We have no doubt we can go to France and prove people wrong again. **JAMIE WARD**

First team coach Stephen Robinson, Roy Carroll and goalkeeping coach Maik Taylor strike a pose.

There have been a few of the young lads like Paddy [McNair] coming in; we joke with each other and I say, 'Ah it's all right for you, just waltz in two years ago, now go to France!" Those lads should have seen Moldova away – that was not so nice! The closest thing I've known is probably when I played in the Europa League final with Fulham and I really loved that night. **AARON HUGHES**

Michael has put a lot of work into the campaign, a lot of good work. We just want to get results and we have the belief. You used to turn up for Northern Ireland and run yourself into the ground. Now we turn up, do that, but with a plan, and a plan people believe in. That's why we have been successful and teams will be wary of us. **GARETH McAULEY**

Whichever group you're in, it is going to be difficult. But you have to look at the qualification process and be confident. We became the first Pot Five team to top their qualifying group and our performances and results merited that. I could not be more proud of the entire squad and staff for delivering this for the supporters. **MICHAEL O'NEILL**

In the campaign I had the most assists in the squad, which showed me I can make an impact at any time when I'm called upon. There have been messages from Derry City and Aberdeen. It's pretty surreal but you have just got to appreciate it. With Scotland not being involved it's been nice to have support not only from Aberdeen but other clubs around Scotland. **NIALL McGINN**

This is the first time we have been here in 30 years and this is for the whole nation, not just us. We want to do everyone proud. For a long time you're travelling to these places and you're thinking "here we go again" and you're losing and so on. But things have finally turned around. We are the best team going into the tournament on form. **CHRIS BAIRD**

Let's get this party started.

FINLAND 1 – 1 NORTHERN IRELAND

The squad point the way to France prior to the game against Finland.

11 October 2015

Olympiastadion, Helsinki

Attendance: 14,550

Qualification was already secured but Michael O'Neill had his sights set on finishing top of the tree. Craig Cathcart scored his first international goal – and earned his dad George money as he had backed his son to score with a £5 bet. It was the perfect start for Northern Ireland when the Watford defender, who had been drafted in to replace the injured Jonny Evans, glanced Niall McGinn's cross into the net. For much of the game it looked as though it would be good enough to seal yet another victory, but the Finns equalised with three minutes left on the clock when defender Paulus Arajuuri pounced for the home side. Mind you, it didn't deny Northern Ireland top spot – or halt another party. The players raced to the fans immediately after the final whistle – two years of hard work had brought the biggest

reward of their careers. Northern Ireland had become the first fifth-seeded side to top their group in European Championship qualifying history. Having won just one game in the World Cup 2014 qualifying campaign, O'Neill's men produced a sensational turnaround to win six, draw three and lose just one of their Euro 2016 qualifiers. Kyle Lafferty wasn't on target in the final game but his seven goals had played a vital role in making sure his side finished top of the pile.

Every single player had written their name in Northern Ireland football history and folklore. All roads and boulevards now led to France.

LINE-UP: McGovern, McNair (McLaughlin 51'), McAuley, Cathcart, Brunt, Davis, Baird, Norwood, McGinn (Ferguson 71'), Lafferty (Magennis 79'), Dallas.

SUBS: McLaughlin, Ferguson, McCullough, McKay, Carroll, McLaughlin, McCourt, Reeves, Ward, Magennis, Boyce, Mannus.

Stuart Dallas takes on the Finland defence.

Craig Cathcart scored Northern Ireland's goal against Finland, ensuring that the team finished at the top of Group F.

I was in a bad way emotionally for a couple of hours after finding out my injury meant I wouldn't play at Euro 2016. You think you're too old to cry but let me assure you I'm not. Michael O'Neill came to see me after my surgery and I just thought I didn't want to let him down and seeing him brought a reality to missing out in the summer and that was tough. Michael trusts me to do a job so I was gutted I wouldn't be there to help him. **CHRIS BRUNT**

The squad were delighted to finish top of their qualifying group.

We always seem to do well against the bigger nations and they're one-off games in the group. I think we need just one win and a draw to get through. Given Michael and the squad he's got, nobody gave us hope to qualify. So why not, why can't we go there and put our mark on the tournament? **OLLIE NORWOOD**

Steven Davis grabs a French flag as he runs towards the Green and White Army to join in the sing-song.

I don't think I have ever enjoyed myself as much in my career. We have real belief in the squad and we want to go to France and show what we are all about and enjoy the tournament. We know the tournament is going to be a step up but we are going to be ready for it. **STEVEN DAVIS**

The Northern Ireland squad, all suited and booted, stand together for a photoshoot at the Culloden Hotel in Cultra on the day that they left for the Euros.

CHAPTER TWO

PREPARING FOR THE ADVENTURE

NORTHERN IRELAND 1 - 0 LATVIA

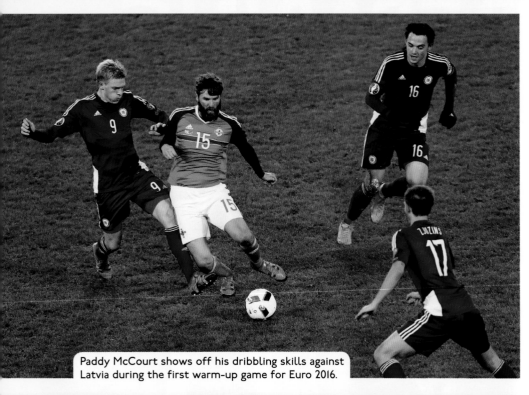

Paddy McCourt shows off his dribbling skills against Latvia during the first warm-up game for Euro 2016.

Chris Baird beats a Latvian player to the ball.

13 November 2015

National Football Stadium at Windsor Park

Attendance: 11,707

There was no let-up for Northern Ireland after qualification. It was straight into warm-up games for the tournament – the first at home against Latvia. Steven Davis scored the decisive goal 10 minutes after half-time as Northern Ireland ended a miserable run of 23 friendly games without a win by beating Latvia. Seventeen of those matches were lost in a run stretching back to March 2008 when they defeated Georgia 4-1. Inspirational captain Davis latched onto a long ball out of defence by Craig Cathcart and fired home the rebound after an initial header was saved by Andris Vaņins. Michael O'Neill's men dominated throughout and extended their unbeaten run to eight matches. It was also an opportunity to experiment a bit with an eye to the summer. 'It was important to keep up the winning momentum and I thought we controlled the game from the first minute to the last,' said O'Neill. 'We changed the system to play three at the back and I was pleased with a lot of aspects of our play.'

LINE-UP: McGovern (Carroll 46'), McAuley, Cathcart, Jonny Evans, Dallas (Ferguson 69'), McLaughlin, Davis (McCourt 84'), Baird, Norwood (Corry Evans 46'), Lafferty (Magennis 54'), Ward (Boyce 69').

SUBS: Ferguson, McGinn, McKay, Boyce, Carroll, Corry Evans, McCourt, Hodson, Magennis, Mannus.

Steven Davis pounces to grab the only goal of the game against Latvia.

Shane Ferguson prepares to deliver a cross.

Liam Boyce questions a decision by one of the officials.

WALES 1 – 1 NORTHERN IRELAND

24 March 2016

Cardiff City Stadium

Attendance: 21,855

Northern Ireland were denied victory by a dubious spot-kick but still claimed a record. Michael O'Neill had led his side on a nine-game unbeaten run – a feat only ever achieved before by the great Billy Bingham, who did it twice, in 1980 and 1985. Craig Cathcart's second-half goal looked as though it was going to give the visitors a rare away friendly win. Amazingly the boys in green had not won a friendly on their travels since 2006. Cathcart, who scored in his second consecutive game after netting in the final qualifier against Finland, wasn't to be the match winner, however. Scottish referee Steven McLean controversially pointed to the spot after Gareth McAuley appeared to get to the ball ahead of Simon Church with a minute left on the clock – and Church slotted home the penalty.

LINE-UP: McGovern, McLaughlin (Hughes 81'), McAuley, Jonny Evans (Daniel Lafferty 73'), Cathcart, Dallas (Ferguson 90+2'), McNair (Paton 73'), Davis, Norwood, Kyle Lafferty (McKay 81'), Washington (Ward 46').

SUBS: Daniel Lafferty, McCullough, McGinn, McKay, Ferguson, Carroll, Hodson, Paton, Hughes, Ward, Carson, Smith.

Conor Washington takes on the Welsh defence.

Steven Davis is tracked by Joe Ledley.

Jamie Ward has an effort pushed away by the Welsh keeper.

Billy McKay is tackled by Welsh defender James Chester.

NORTHERN IRELAND 1 – 0 SLOVENIA

Conor Washington opened his account for Northern Ireland with a well-taken goal

Kyle Lafferty has an aerial duel with a Slovenian defender.

Shane Ferguson is pushed off the ball.

28 March 2016

National Football Stadium at Windsor Park

Attendance: 13,500

Conor Washington was born in England to a Scottish mother and lived in Wales – but in this game he announced himself as a fully-fledged Ulsterman. The new hero had never been to his adopted football home of the National Football Stadium at Windsor Park until just days before his debut. But the former postman delivered a first-class parcel to seal a narrow win over Slovenia and ensure Michael O'Neill's men stretched their unbeaten run to 10 games and broke their record in style. 'Scoring a goal on my home debut, it doesn't get much better than that,' said the Queens Park Rangers striker. 'It's one of the highlights of my career. It was an incredible experience, a fairy tale. The atmosphere was unbelievable and that was with only three sides of the ground finished.' The win – Northern Ireland's 150th in international football – was secured thanks to Roy Carroll's terrific second-half penalty save to deny Milivoje Novaković.

LINE-UP: Carroll, McAuley (Hughes 46'), Evans, Cathcart, Smith (McLaughlin 71'), McNair (McGinn 79'), Davis, Norwood, Ferguson (Dallas 60'), Ward (Kyle Lafferty 60'), Washington (Magennis 70').

SUBS: Hughes, McKay, Daniel Lafferty, McLaughlin, Magennis, Kyle Lafferty, Hodson, McCullough, McGovern, McGinn, Paton, Dallas.

Jonny Evans gets measured up for his suit.

Belfast menswear retailer Bogart teamed up with iconic London brand Herbie Frogg to supply the official Northern Ireland team suit for Euro 2016. Here Paddy McNair, Gareth McAuley, Jonny Evans and Ollie Norwood take part in the official suit photoshoot.

Gareth McAuley fixes his tie during his suit fitting.

Gareth McAuley and Jonny Evans getting dressed to impress.

Bogart's John Keenan helps Ollie Norwood to tie the perfect knot.

NORTHERN IRELAND 3 – 0 BELARUS

27 May 2016

National Football Stadium at Windsor Park

Attendance: 14,229

'Will Grigg's On Fire', based on dance track 'Freed From Desire' by Gala (1996), dominated the build-up to Euro 2016, not to mention becoming the unofficial anthem of the finals in France. And Grigg was certainly hotting up after making a cameo appearance from the bench. The Wigan Athletic striker ensured 14,000-odd people went home happy. Sub Niall McGinn crossed from the right and when keeper Andrey Gorbunov punched the ball into his path a nation held its breath. Grigg was the most confident man in Belfast, however, as he hammered low into the net to raise the roof. First-half goals from Kyle Lafferty and Conor Washington had already put Michael O'Neill's men two up. Fireworks got the after-match party started and with Grigg on fire there had to be flames in the mix. After retreating to the dressing room briefly, the players came back out to receive the acclaim of the ecstatic fans.

LINE-UP: Carroll (Mannus 46'), McLaughlin, Baird, Jonny Evans, Cathcart, Dallas (Hughes 74'), McNair, Davis (Norwood 46'), Corry Evans (McGinn 74'), Lafferty (Grigg 61'), Washington (Ward 61').

SUBS: Hodson, McAuley, McGinn, Grigg, Mannus, McCullough, Norwood, Hughes, Ward, Magennis, McGovern.

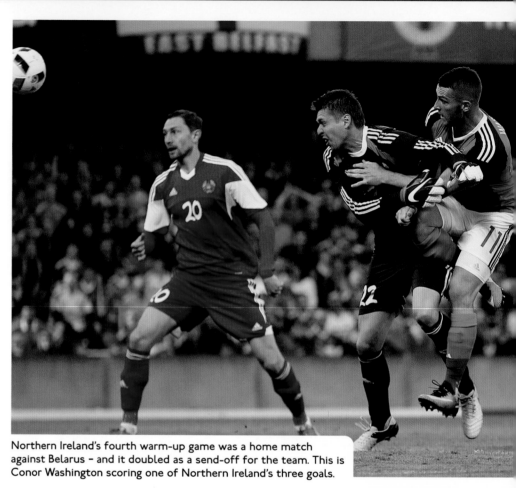

Northern Ireland's fourth warm-up game was a home match against Belarus – and it doubled as a send-off for the team. This is Conor Washington scoring one of Northern Ireland's three goals.

Members of the squad enjoy the party at the National Football Stadium at Windsor Park at the end of May.

You would think from Dave Cavan's picture that Will Grigg really was on fire that night!

Jonny Evans tussles with a Belarus forward during the game.

There was a pyrotechnics display at the stadium as part of the send-off.

Northern Ireland's players were pretty much household names up and down the country before Euro 2016 but their faces were to become instantly recognisable too before they flew to France.

The Irish FA commissioned giant billboards featuring the Northern Ireland squad and manager Michael O'Neill which were erected throughout the country as excitement reached fever pitch. The billboards featured images of the 30 players hoping to be on the plane to France and had the unique twist of being made up of a mosaic of thousands of photographs of the Green and White Army. With representatives from every county in Northern Ireland selected in the extended squad, the billboards also featured the names of players' home towns. From Kesh to Cookstown and Bangor to Portadown, the giant posters were displayed in or close to the part of the country where each player grew up. Those players eligible for selection through ancestry weren't forgotten; eye-catching images of the likes of Jamie Ward, Oliver Norwood and Conor Washington were displayed on billboard poster sites across Belfast. Jim Shaw, the then Irish FA President, said, 'These billboards are a fantastic way of showcasing the players as the heroes that they are. Each one is a work of art in itself and they really demonstrate in a dynamic way that every part of Northern Ireland will be represented when the team runs onto the pitch in France.'

A two-week billboard advertising campaign featuring Northern Ireland players – and urging support for the boys in green – ran prior to the team's participation at Euro 2016. Many of the billboards were displayed in the players' home towns. The campaign was officially launched at the James Wray & Company Gallery in central Belfast. Here Adrian Beattie of Navigator Blue, the company that created the images used in the campaign from thousands of pictures sent in by fans, checks out Michael O'Neill's billboard as Luke McCullough and Liam Boyce look on.

An exhibition at the James Wray & Company Gallery of the images that appeared on billboards.

In the shadow of a DeLorean convention at Titanic Belfast, Michael O'Neill named the 23 players who would take Northern Ireland back to the future.

O'Neill announced his travelling party in front of 400 invited guests and fans at a glitzy event as the enormity of what he had achieved with the Class of '16 became real. Stars of previous glory years such as 1958 World Cup hero Peter McParland and iconic goalkeeper Pat Jennings, who played at the 1982 and 1986 World Cups, spoke to MC Colin Murray on stage before O'Neill got down to the business of revealing the names of the players who would carry the hopes of a nation. Having waited 30 long years, the Irish FA made sure it was a day to remember with an innovative and eye-catching way of announcing the news to the world. Prior to the event, London-based company Projection Artworks was commissioned to project images of the players onto the world-famous basalt pillars at the Giant's

Causeway in County Antrim – and a film featuring the projections rolled as Michael O'Neill announced the names of the players who had made the cut for France. O'Neill had told the players who would be packing their bags for France in advance but insisted the likes of Liam Boyce, who missed out, would still have a

huge part to play in his country's future. O'Neill said: 'I probably knew who would be on the plane when we were at our training camp in Manchester. It was important they knew in advance but missing out on the Euros does not mean an end to their international careers in the slightest.'

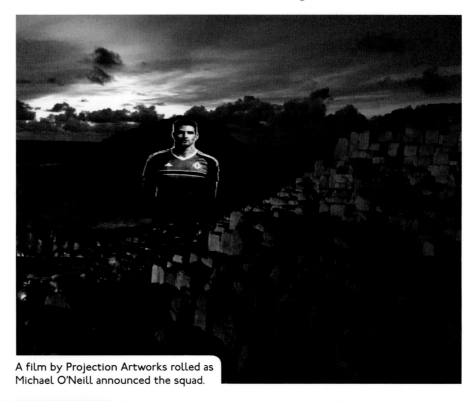

A film by Projection Artworks rolled as Michael O'Neill announced the squad.

The official squad announcement for Euro 2016 was staged at Titanic Belfast. Hundreds of Northern Ireland's top fans were invited along.

Broadcaster Colin Murray, the MC, chats with Michael O'Neill about his hopes for the tournament.

'Standing on the Shoulders of Giants' was the theme for the squad announcement, which featured some giants of Northern Ireland football. At the official photoshoot Michael O'Neill was joined by Peter McParland who represented the team that competed at the World Cup in Sweden in 1958, while Billy Hamilton and Pat Jennings represented the Spain '82 and Mexico '86 World Cup squads respectively.

Michael O'Neill and Steven Davis join the squad at Belfast City Airport as they get ready to board their charter flight to Austria for a training camp before travelling on to Slovakia for a final warm-up game prior to the European Championship finals in France.

Stuart Dallas heads for the plane.

Michael McGovern and Niall McGinn on the tarmac.

The captains meet ... Steven Davis with the captain of the charter plane.

The Fire and Rescue Unit at Belfast City Airport provided a special send-off for the team.

SLOVAKIA 0 – 0 NORTHERN IRELAND

Northern Ireland and Slovakia line up at the City Arena.

After the final whistle Aaron Hughes was congratulated by team administrator David Currie on earning his 100th cap for his country during the match.

Aaron Hughes acknowledges the fans' applause.

The players presented Aaron with a special team shirt on earning his 100th cap.

4 June 2016

Stadion Antona Malatinskeho (City Arena), Trnava

Attendance: 18,111

The most important thing was to leave Trnava for Lyon with a clean bill of health and Michael O'Neill was able to breathe a sigh of relief after the 90 minutes. Without a doubt the highlight of this encounter was Aaron Hughes becoming Northern Ireland's second – and first outfield – centurion. The experienced defender and former captain had come full circle having made his debut as a fresh-faced 18-year-old against Slovenia in 1998. He said, 'I can't describe it. It was a little bit emotional making a speech in the dressing room after the game. I've received a lot of good wishes this week and I was trying to play it down a bit because I just wanted to get onto the pitch. I'm going to the Euros because of these lads. I can look back on the 100 caps as a personal thing and it was always going to be a big thing but the Euros is bigger. I retired when I did because I was disillusioned thinking it was never going to be possible. Now that it has happened it is incredible. To still be part of this group has made it special for me.'

LINE-UP: McGovern, Cathcart (Hughes 30'), McAuley, Jonny Evans, McNair (McLaughlin 90+1'), Ferguson (Hodson 86'), Davis, Baird, Norwood (Corry Evans 84'), Lafferty (Washington 55'), Ward (Magennis 46').

SUBS: Carroll, Mannus, McLaughlin, McGinn, Grigg, Washington, Corry Evans, McCullough, Hughes, Magennis, Hodson.

After months of exhaustive research Michael O'Neill settled on the small sports complex at Parc de Montchervet in the town of Saint-Georges-de-Reneins, north of Lyon, as the team's training base for Euro 2016 and the nearby Château de Pizay as the team hotel. The players quickly settled into their surroundings in France and, as this picture shows, got down to work.

EURO2016

CHAPTER THREE

BEHIND THE
SCENES

As soon as the Northern Ireland squad touched down on French soil, they realised that great care had been taken to ensure that France would feel like a home away from home for them and the backroom staff.

The governing body had made sure that no one would be pining for home comforts at the Château de Pizay base outside Lyon. It meant a lot to the players, as Chris Baird explained: 'When you walk into your bedroom, just above the telly you've got the final group table and your picture beside it. And then pictures of our families are there. I've got pictures of my wife and two kids in a bedside frame. Your name is on towels – just little things like that. But seeing the family side of things was really nice because I hadn't seen them in a long time. It just makes it seem a bit more homely. We didn't expect it. There is no risk of us getting bored, though. Around the hotel there's so many things for us to do anyway. Some people might like to be by themselves; the majority of us like to be in the games room where there are pool tables and dartboards.'

The locals also played their part in making sure Michael O'Neill's men were happy in their surroundings. Shop windows in the area had Northern Ireland flags painted on them, flags flew from lamp posts and hundreds of schoolchildren and their families attended an open training session. Security was, of course, tight. Armed guards and sniffer dogs created a ring of steel around the team hotel 24/7. O'Neill has been Northern Ireland's greatest leader in years and he was made to feel like royalty. A keen jogger, he wasn't allowed to run without close security tracking his every move, though that didn't seem to trouble him at all: 'Security is very tight. It has a bit of a presidential feel to it, which I've kind of enjoyed. The base we have is fantastic for the players because I'm staying at the other end of the hotel. It's perfect for them – I get a bit of peace and they get peace from me as well.'

One behind-the-scenes moment that stood out for O'Neill occurred after Northern Ireland were defeated by Wales and the squad took a fancy for fast food: 'Coming away from the Wales game on the bus, the players were pleading with me to let them stop at a McDonald's. They'd behaved like monks the whole tournament, eating nothing but pasta and rice, so they deserved it. But we had to get our security guy up the front of the coach to okay this unscheduled stop. He got nicknamed Jason Bourne because of how he whispered into a microphone up his sleeve. We were given the all clear but basically this small town [Belleville] had to be shut down for us. Thirty policemen manned roadblocks and five guards with machine guns delivered the Big Macs.'

Michael O'Neill and Irish FA President Jim Shaw step off the plane at Lyon Airport as French dignitaries wait to greet them.

Shane Ferguson, Roy Carroll, Alan Mannus and Will Grigg get ready to set foot on French soil after jetting in from Slovakia.

Craig Stanfield, the Irish FA's logistics and venue operations manager, removes some of the 'welcome' props used for the team's arrival in France.

Players board the team bus - it became a familiar sight on the roads north of Lyon during Northern Ireland's stay in France.

There was a heavy security presence at the Château de Pizay hotel, which was the team's base camp in France.

The players line up to get the keys to their rooms, which were in an annexe of the main hotel.

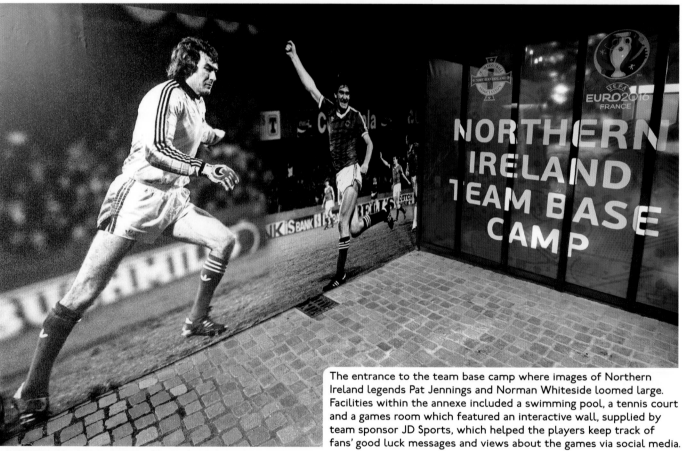

The entrance to the team base camp where images of Northern Ireland legends Pat Jennings and Norman Whiteside loomed large. Facilities within the annexe included a swimming pool, a tennis court and a games room which featured an interactive wall, supplied by team sponsor JD Sports, which helped the players keep track of fans' good luck messages and views about the games via social media.

The Château de Pizay is in a picturesque setting, surrounded by vineyards.

Irish FA President Jim Shaw organised a meal for the squad, the media, backroom staff and other support staff as well as officials from the local municipality in the impressive Castle Café within Château de Bagnols at Le Bourg, Bagnols.

Among the guests at the meal in Bagnols was the mayor of the municipality of Saint-Georges-de-Reneins, Sylvie Epinat, who posed for a picture with Michael O'Neill.

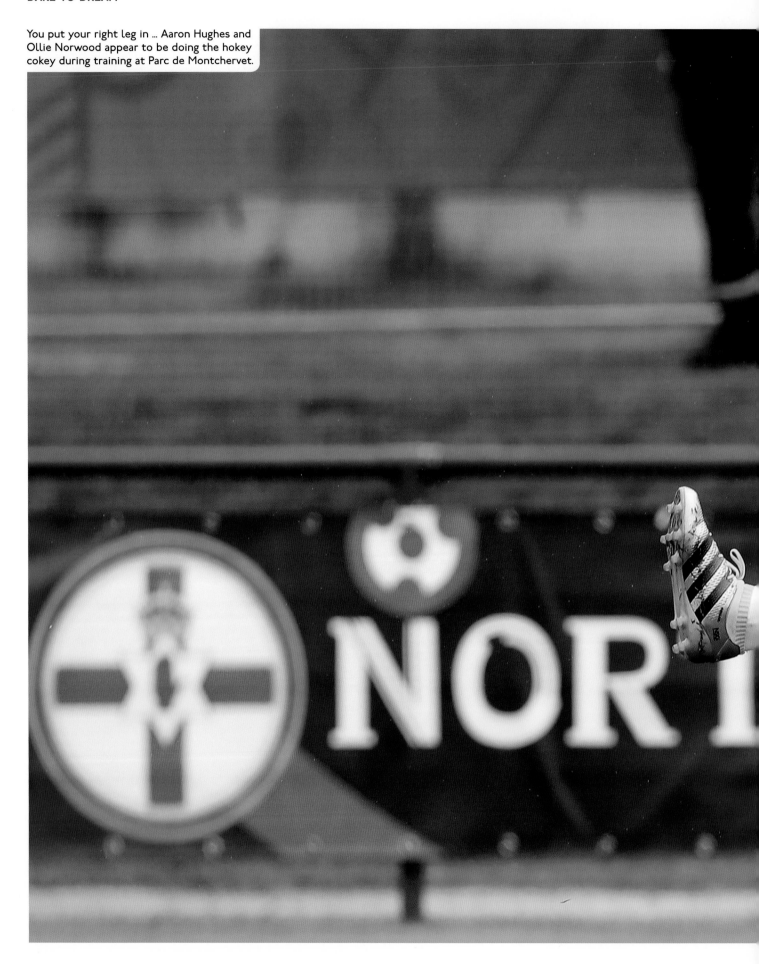

You put your right leg in ... Aaron Hughes and Ollie Norwood appear to be doing the hokey cokey during training at Parc de Montchervet.

The Northern Ireland players often personalise their boots by putting their own names or their children's names on them.

Michael O'Neill's meticulous preparation of the team along with detailed analysis of the opposition were big factors in Northern Ireland reaching the European Championship finals for the first time in the country's history. His attention to detail was again evident on the training pitch at Parc de Montchervet.

Assistant manager Jimmy Nicholl and first team coach Stephen Robinson talk tactics with Michael O'Neill.

The international boss in contemplative mood.

The Irish FA invited the people of the Saint-Georges-de-Reneins area to watch the players train at Parc de Montchervet. The ticketed event attracted hundreds of locals.

Paddy McNair and Will Grigg sign autographs at the event.

Some of the players got an unexpected soaking at one of the training sessions when a sprinkler was turned on by mistake.

A media centre, sponsored by Tourism Ireland, was set up in a community complex adjacent to the training ground. It featured a press conference room and a media working room as well as TV interview rooms. And the walls were adorned with pictures of both the players and Northern Ireland landmarks. Here Kyle Lafferty encounters a familiar face as he enters the centre.

A reporter trains live video-streaming app Periscope on Michael O'Neill and Neil Brittain, the Irish FA's head of communications.

Chris Baird and Ollie Norwood are introduced to the media by Nigel Tilson, senior media officer at the Irish FA.

Michael O'Neill faces questions from the press.

Under-21 players Joel Cooper (right) and Paul Smyth (centre) were invited by Michael O'Neill to train with the squad in France – to give them a taste of what it is like to be a senior international taking part in a major tourney.

Kyle Lafferty and Jonny Evans working hard in training.

Craig Cathcart takes a break from working out in the gym.

Aaron Hughes, Michael McGovern, Chris Brunt, Jamie Ward, Josh Magennis and Gareth McAuley check out the sights during a players' walkabout in Saint-Georges-de-Reneins.

Aaron Hughes tickles a friendly pooch.

Josh Magennis, Stuart Dallas and Lee Hodson jump for joy in training.

Michael McGovern at full stretch.

Kyle Lafferty shows off his jumping skills.

Michael O'Neill prepares to put the players through their paces.

Michael McGovern decided to go for a haircut after training one day. At the salon he was shown books featuring hairstyles mainly from the '70s and '80s – not the looks he wanted! Thanks to his smartphone – plus the international language of hand gestures – he was able to explain the type of cut he required and emerged beautifully coiffed.

The Irish FA's digital team went into overdrive during the tournament. Their videos, tweets and Facebook posts enjoyed a remarkable number of views during June, including 3.9 million minutes of video content watched and 28.3 million impressions on Twitter. The team also managed to attract 90,000 new followers on social media channels. One of the most popular videos featured some of the players phoning home to thank fans for their support and to wish them a safe journey to France. It was viewed by 473,000 people. Here Steven Davis and Josh Magennis talk to a supporter.

Aaron Hughes chats with a fan.

Assistant manager Jimmy Nicholl on the blower.

Several celebrity fans joined the Green and White Army in France. They included golf superstar Rory McIlroy, who also produced an inspirational video for the players which was shown to them prior to the tournament. It was later posted on social media and was viewed by millions of people around the world. Here he is enjoying a laugh with the squad.

Rory at the Germany game in Paris chatting to Michael McGovern and Northern Ireland Deputy First Minister Martin McGuinness shortly after the team arrived at the ground.

David Currie, the team admin manager, grabs a picture of Michael O'Neill and Rory beside the Paris Saint-Germain crest in the changing rooms at Parc des Princes.

Security was also tight at the training ground.

Corry Evans and Conor McLaughlin compete for the ball during training.

Michael O'Neill and assistant coach/analyst Austin MacPhee discuss tactics with the players.

Austin MacPhee and Michael McGovern analyse the keeper's performances.

Ollie Norwood in reflective mood at Parc de Montchervet.

Chris Baird relaxes at Château de Pizay.

Chris Baird strikes a serious pose –
and has a laugh – beside one of the
statues at the team hotel.

It was blue skies all the way when Northern faced Poland at Stade de Nice, the venue for Northern Ireland's first-ever game at a European Championship finals.

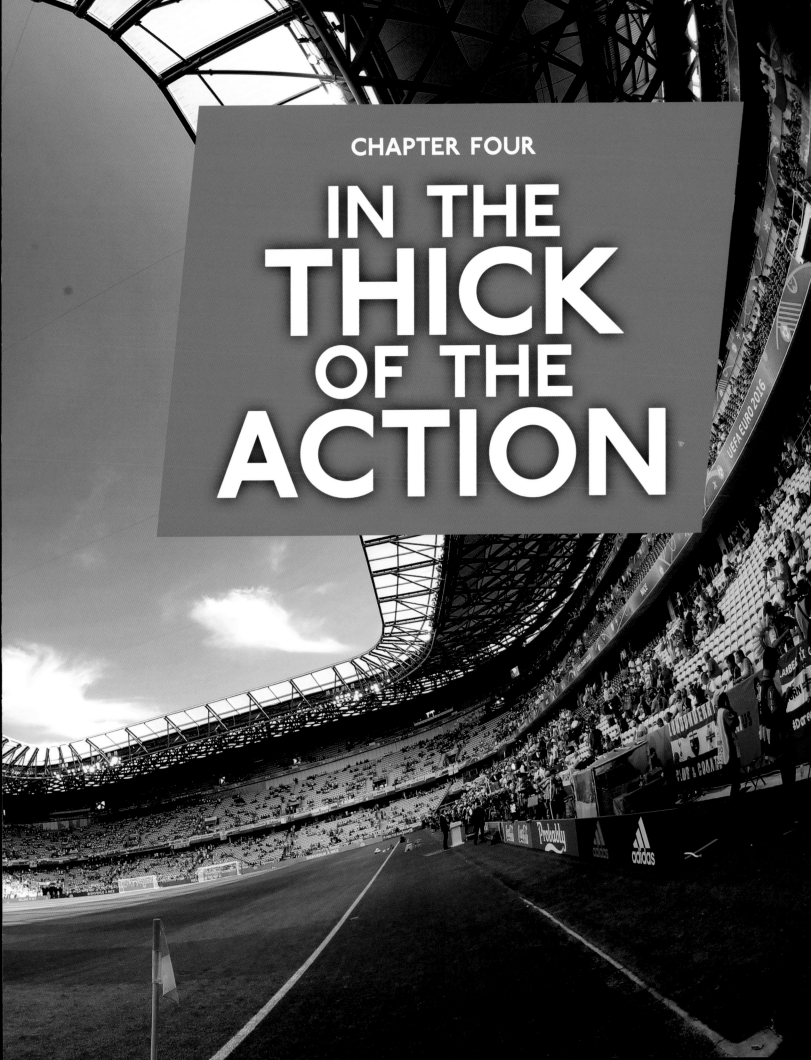

CHAPTER FOUR

IN THE THICK OF THE ACTION

POLAND 1 - 0 NORTHERN IRELAND

12 June 2016 - Group C

Poland 1-0 Northern Ireland

Milik 51'

Stade de Nice, Nice

Attendance: 33,742 (including 10,000 Northern Ireland fans)

Referee: Ovidiu Haţegan (Romania)

The day Northern Ireland fans and players had been waiting 30 years to experience had finally arrived. All roads led to the picturesque setting of the Côte d'Azur as Nice was painted green and white for the day. Captain Steven Davis made history as Northern Ireland became the first team in Europe to take advantage of a change to the laws of the game by taking part in a one-man kick-off in the match against Poland. 'UEFA spoke to us and

said about rule changes and it was something we were going to do in the Slovakia [warm-up] game,' said Davis. 'The referee said no at that point. We didn't give it too much thought but the reason was to get an extra player out wide from kick-off. As far as Kyle goes, he was the target for the next ball. I believe we were one of the first teams to do it. I think there was a team in the Copa America who did it so it is a little piece of history [in Europe].'

Northern Ireland's Euro 2016 campaign got off to a losing start as Arkadiusz Milik scored the only goal of the game at the Stade de Nice, ending a stunning 12-game unbeaten run. Gareth McAuley left an early calling card on Milik within the first minute but the Poles attacked with pace and purpose. For 10 minutes McAuley was touch-tight on dangerman Robert Lewandowski, never giving him a kick, a tale that

continued throughout the game. It was a huge let-off when Bartosz Kapustka rifled a strike from 25 yards but Michael McGovern got both palms on it to divert the effort over the bar. Northern Ireland needed to hear the half-time whistle to regroup and rethink.

In the second half, on came Stuart Dallas for Paddy McNair and O'Neill switched to a back three, with Jonny Evans shifted to the left. That was the formation, if not the personnel, that had served them so well in qualifying and they immediately looked more comfortable. But just when it looked as though Northern Ireland were beginning to get a footing in the game the Poles struck. Jakub Błaszczykowski picked out Ajax striker Milik and he made no mistake with a low strike to McGovern's left – the keeper had no chance.

Northern Ireland's starting line-up against the Poles.

Conor Washington, who had netted twice in his first four internationals, replaced Shane Ferguson as O'Neill went for it. Kyle Lafferty fired an ambitious overhead kick high, wide and not so handsome from 20 yards, and that was as close as they came to levelling.

It wasn't the start anyone had imagined, but the dream was far from over. 'No one likes to lose football games,' said defender Jonny Evans after the match. 'As much as we've enjoyed the experience, when it came to it we lost our first game. It was against a good side, a team that controlled the game and made it very difficult for us. We can't let the Ukraine game pass us by. We need to be more proactive in the game. We will settle ourselves down a bit. There were times that you got caught up in the adrenaline of it all so maybe we should compose ourselves a bit more.'

Michael O'Neill and some of his backroom staff – including physiotherapist Darren McMaster, head physio Caroline Woods, team doctor David White, team administration manager David Currie, coach and analyst Austin MacPhee, goalkeeping coach Maik Taylor and first team coach Stephen Robinson – stand for the anthems.

Conor Washington is stopped in his tracks by Polish keeper Wojciech Szczęsny.

Craig Cathcart outjumps Polish captain and talisman Robert Lewandowski.

Shane Ferguson is tackled by Poland's Jakub Błaszczykowski.

Michael O'Neill in the dugout during the game.

NORTHERN IRELAND LINE-UP

1   Michael McGovern

2   Conor McLaughlin

20   Craig Cathcart

5   Jonny Evans

4   Gareth McAuley

17   Paddy McNair
     (Stuart Dallas 46′)

3   Shane Ferguson
     (Conor Washington 66′)

16   Oliver Norwood

8   Steven Davis (c)

6   Chris Baird
     (Jamie Ward 76′)

10   Kyle Lafferty

SUBSTITUTES

7   Niall McGinn

9   Will Grigg

11   Conor Washington

12   Roy Carroll

13   Corry Evans

14   Stuart Dallas

15   Luke McCullough

18   Aaron Hughes

19   Jamie Ward

21   Josh Magennis

22   Lee Hodson

23   Alan Mannus

Gareth McAuley is outmuscled by the Polish defence.

The Northern Ireland players look dejected after the Poles grab the only goal of the game through Arkadiusz Milik.

Conor McLaughlin chests the ball as Poland winger Bartosz Kapustka closes in.

Jamie Ward battles for possession with Grzegorz Krychowiak.

Michael O'Neill keeps an eye on the action in Stade de Nice.

Polish defender Krzysztof Mączyński gets to grips with Ollie Norwood.

A familiar sight during Euro 2016 ... Jonny Evans clears the danger.

POLAND LINE-UP

1   Wojciech Szczesny

20 Łukasz Piszczek

15 Kamil Glik

2   Michał Pazdan

3   Artur Jędrzeczyk

16 Jakub Błaszczykowski
    (Kamil Grosicki 80')

10 Grzegorz Krychowiak

5   Krzysztof Mączyński
    (Tomasz Jodłowiec 78')

21 Bartosz Kapustka
    (Sławomir Peszko 88')

7   Arkadiusz Milik

9   Robert Lewandowski (c)

Manager: Adam Nawałka

SUBSTITUTES

4   Thiago Cionek

6   Tomasz Jodłowiec

8   Karol Linetty

11 Kamil Grosicki

12 Artur Boruc

13 Mariusz Stępiński

14 Jakub Wawrzyniak

17 Sławomir Peszko

18 Bartosz Salamon

19 Piotr Zieliński

22 Łukasz Fabiański

23 Filip Starzyński

Kyle Lafferty traps the ball with a Polish defender in close proximity.

Jamie Ward shakes the hand of Grzegorz Krychowiak at the final whistle.

UKRAINE 0 – 2 NORTHERN IRELAND

16 June 2016 - Group C

Ukraine 0-2 Northern Ireland

McAuley 49', McGinn 90+6'

Parc Olympique Lyonnais (Stade de Lyon), Lyon

Attendance: 51,043 (including 16,000 Northern Ireland fans)

Referee: Pavel Královec (Czech Republic)

Thunder, lightning and hail sprayed the Stade de Lyon but it was Northern Ireland that were now causing a storm. Second-half goals from Gareth McAuley and substitute Niall McGinn gave Michael O'Neill's men a much-needed 2-0 win to keep their dreams of a place in the knockout stages alive. It was a sublime performance from start to finish, showing heart, determination and class in equal measure. Led by a manager with a masterplan, Northern Ireland created history by securing their first ever European Championship finals victory.

Experienced defender Aaron Hughes, who had become his country's first outfield centurion a week earlier, was one of five bold changes made by the manager after the defeat to Poland. Everyone knew that the showdown with Ukraine was a make-or-break tussle and a defeat would probably lead to Northern Ireland being the first nation to be eliminated from the tournament.

From the off the boys in green were on top but the match remained goalless until four minutes into the second half when the roof was almost taken off the Stade de Lyon by the rejoicing of the Green and White Army. Taking a free-kick, Ollie Norwood spotted

Stade de Lyon – the venue for Northern Ireland's second Group C game against Ukraine.

The starting 11 against Ukraine.

a run from Gareth McAuley and the West Brom man got away from his marker to direct his header across goal and into the far corner. It was McAuley's eighth international strike – the highest number ever by a defender in a Northern Ireland shirt and every one of them from a set-piece move, which have become so crucial to the success enjoyed under O'Neill.

As if the goal didn't cause enough drama, referee Pavel Královec sparked bizarre scenes when he halted play for four minutes after a heavy hailstorm pelted the pitch. Not that it made any difference to the winning form of Northern Ireland. Between Michael McGovern and his defence there was simply

no way through for Ukraine – and it was about to get even better. Substitute Josh Magennis showed great feet before pulling the ball back for Stuart Dallas. His shot was parried and Niall McGinn proved to be a super sub yet again by slamming the ball into the net to complete a memorable victory.

'We've come here, reacted to the Poland defeat, got three points and it gives us a realistic chance to get something from the Germany game and get ourselves out of the group,' said McAuley. 'People maybe didn't give us a chance and said we wouldn't get a point, so it's always nice to turn the screw and prove a few people wrong. To me that's what Northern Ireland is about. It's

about being the underdog, scrapping and fighting. The most pleasing thing is that it was a Northern Ireland performance out there.'

McGinn's family weren't in Lyon to witness his moment of glory; his dad had gone home after a week in Nice and his mum had had to go back for his sister Paula's hen party. But even that didn't take the shine off what was a magic moment: 'It was just the best night of my career, by far. To hit the net in an international tournament is just out of this world. When I switched on my phone it went crazy. The amount of messages was phenomenal. My Facebook page and Twitter went crazy.'

NORTHERN IRELAND LINE-UP

 1   Michael McGovern
18   Aaron Hughes
20   Craig Cathcart
 4   Gareth McAuley
 5   Jonny Evans
19   Jamie Ward
     (Niall McGinn 69')
13   Corry Evans (Paddy
     McNair 90+3')
 8   Steven Davis (c)
16   Oliver Norwood
14   Stuart Dallas
11   Conor Washington
     (Josh Magennis 84')

SUBSTITUTES
 2   Conor McLaughlin
 3   Shane Ferguson
 6   Chris Baird
 7   Niall McGinn
 9   Will Grigg
10   Kyle Lafferty
12   Roy Carroll
15   Luke McCullough
17   Paddy McNair
21   Josh Magennis
22   Lee Hodson
23   Alan Mannus

Gareth McAuley's towering header from an Ollie Norwood free-kick flies past Ukrainian keeper Andriy Pyatov to put Northern Ireland one up.

Gareth McAuley celebrates his famous goal – the first ever scored by a Northern Ireland player at a European Championship finals – along with Jonny Evans, Conor Washington and Craig Cathcart.

Gareth McAuley was mobbed by his team-mates after finding the back of the net.

UKRAINE LINE-UP

12 Andriy Pyatov

17 Artem Fedetskyi

3 Yevhen Khacheridi

20 Yaroslav Rakitskiy

13 Vyacheslav Shevchuk (c)

16 Serhiy Sydorchuk
    (Denys Garmash 76')

6 Taras Stepanenko

7 Andriy Yarmolenko

9 Viktor Kovalenko
   (Oleksandr Zinchenko
   83')

10 Yevhen Konoplyanka

11 Yevhen Seleznyov
    (Roman Zozulya 71')

Manager: Mykhaylo
Fomenko

SUBSTITUTES

1 Denys Boyko

2 Bohdan Butko

4 Anatoliy Tymoshchuk

5 Olexandr Kucher

8 Roman Zozulya

14 Ruslan Rotan

15 Pylyp Budkivskiy

18 Serhiy Rybalka

19 Denys Garmash

21 Oleksandr Zinchenko

22 Oleksandr Karavaev

23 Mykyta Shevchenko

Aaron Hughes closes in on Ukraine's Yevhen Konoplyanka.

Steven Davis attempts to take the ball off Yaroslav Rakitskiy.

Corry Evans beats Taras Stepanenko to the ball.

Jamie Ward races away from Ukrainian midfielder Viktor Kovalenko.

Conor Washington receives some close attention from Yevhen Khacheridi.

The Ukrainian defence climb all over Gareth McAuley during the game in Stade de Lyon.

Jonny Evans goes airborne in the driving rain.

Niall McGinn is in dreamland after scoring Northern Ireland's second goal against Ukraine deep into injury time.

Josh Magennis and Niall McGinn celebrate the winner.

Jonny Evans was pretty emotional at the final whistle.

Michael McGovern, Gareth McAuley and Kyle Lafferty are delighted with the now famous win.

Aaron Hughes applauds the Green and White Army. Around 16,000 Northern Ireland fans were in the stadium that day.

Two more players - this time Jamie Ward and Stuart Dallas - are as pleased as punch.

Gareth McAuley was voted man of the match for his performance against the Ukrainians.

NORTHERN IRELAND 0 – 1 GERMANY

The players warm up before their training session at the home of Paris Saint-Germain, where Ulsterman Jonathan Calderwood is the head groundsman.

21 June 2016 – Group C

Northern Ireland 0-1 Germany

Gómez 30'

Parc des Princes, Paris

Attendance: 44,125 (including 10,000 Northern Ireland fans)

Referee: Clement Turpin (France)

In the game against Germany Michael McGovern upstaged the world's best keeper, Manuel Neuer, with a truly heroic display at the Parc des Princes. The Northern Ireland keeper made a magnificent seven stunning saves to ensure his country qualified for the last 16 as one of the best third-placed sides after a gutsy, stubborn and quality defensive display. The Green and White Army were in no doubt about their destiny as they chanted 'We're Not Going Home' before kick-off.

McGovern was finally beaten by Mario Gomez's first-half effort but it took a deflection to find a way past the man who would be on the shopping list of a host of clubs after the tournament. Thomas Müller cursed the reactions of the keeper as well as hitting the woodwork twice and McGovern produced super saves to deny the Marios – Gómez and Götze. Mesut Özil also failed to find a way past the Fermanagh man as McGovern produced the most commanding display of goalkeeping seen at Euro 2016. 'I really enjoyed it, I enjoyed the challenge and I enjoyed the other two games as well and the tournament has been even better than I could have imagined,' said the heroic keeper.

He added, 'Even before the first game and second game I felt confident and relaxed ... I wasn't one bit nervous. There were no

Michael O'Neill gathers his thoughts as Northern Ireland train in Parc des Princes ahead of the final Group C game against world champions Germany.

Steven Davis helps Chris Baird with his stretching exercises.

The Northern Ireland bench stand for the anthems in Paris.

The 11 who started the game against Germany, aka Die Mannschaft (The Team), at Euro 2016.

butterflies in my stomach, which was unusual. I just knew that I had prepared the best I could and I was ready to give it my best shot and if it wasn't good enough then it wasn't good enough, but I was confident in my own ability that I could do well. It was difficult, especially in the opening part of the game. Getting through is the ultimate thing. We have enjoyed this experience so much we really don't want to go home yet and seeing the fans tonight I don't think they want to go home either. The boys gave me a round of applause when I came in and I was a bit embarrassed, but obviously it was really nice. I have got so much respect for all the boys in the dressing room – they are great boys – so it was a nice touch.'

McGovern was finally beaten on the half hour – Muller was forced slightly wide by Jonny Evans but he produced a clever lay-off for Gomez, who rifled in from 8 yards thanks to a deflection off McAuley which took it over McGovern.

The Germans were relentless for the rest of the match. It was nerve-tingling stuff but O'Neill's men were hanging in there – thanks in the main to the magical McGovern. Skipper Steven Davis knew that the keeper was key to his side making it through to the knockout stages: 'Michael's performance was definitely one of the best goalkeeping displays I've seen. We knew it was likely that they were going to get opportunities but he just seemed to be there every time. We had the belief that if they did get through he was going to save us. Michael is a very level-headed guy; I don't want to disrespect the club he's at, but he definitely should be playing at a higher level. Anybody watching that tonight couldn't help but be impressed by his performance, likewise the first two games. He's been brilliant.'

Michael McGovern made a string of wonder saves against Germany, including this one at Mario Götze's feet.

Steven Davis keeps Germany's Mesut Özil at bay.

Kyle Lafferty tackles Bastian Schweinsteiger.

Jamie Ward pings the ball as Mario Götze closes in.

German defender Mats Hummels challenges Conor Washington.

NORTHERN IRELAND LINE-UP

1 Michael McGovern
18 Aaron Hughes
4 Gareth McAuley
20 Craig Cathcart
5 Jonny Evans
8 Steven Davis (c)
19 Jamie Ward
    (Josh Magennis 70')
13 Corry Evans
    (Niall McGinn 84')
16 Oliver Norwood
14 Stuart Dallas
11 Conor Washington
    (Kyle Lafferty 59')

SUBSTITUTES

2 Conor McLaughlin
3 Shane Ferguson
6 Chris Baird
7 Niall McGinn
9 Will Grigg
10 Kyle Lafferty
12 Roy Carroll
15 Luke McCullough
17 Paddy McNair
21 Josh Magennis
22 Lee Hodson
23 Alan Mannus

GERMANY LINE-UP

1 Manuel Neuer (c)
21 Joshua Kimmich
17 Jérôme Boateng
    (Benedikt Höwedes 76')
5 Mats Hummels
3 Jonas Hector
6 Sami Khedira (Bastian
    Schweinsteiger 69')
18 Toni Kroos
8 Mesut Özil
13 Thomas Müller
19 Mario Götze
    (André Schürrle 55')
23 Mario Gómez
Manager: Joachim Löw

SUBSTITUTES

2 Shkodran Mustafi
4 Benedikt Höwedes
7 Bastian Schweinsteiger
9 André Schürrle
10 Lukas Podolski
11 Julian Draxler
12 Bernd Leno
14 Emre Can
15 Julian Weigl
16 Jonathan Tah
20 Leroy Sané
22 Marc-André ter Stegen

Corry Evans, Ollie Norwood and
Mesut Özil try a spot of ball juggling.

Stuart Dallas, Steven Davis and Aaron Hughes applaud the Northern Ireland fans at the end of the match in Paris. Around 10,000 of them watched the game.

Jonny Evans at the final whistle.

The players wait in the VIP terminal at Charles de Gaulle Airport in Paris for their charter flight back to Lyon after the game against Germany. They were boarding the bus to the plane when they heard that their result against the world champions was enough to put them into the Round of 16 as one of the best third-placed teams in the groups.

Michael McGovern and Niall McGinn are all smiles after hearing the team have cemented their place in the next stage of Euro 2016. We'll say nothing about the joker behind them!

WALES 1 – 0 NORTHERN IRELAND

25 June 2016 – Round of 16

Wales 1-0 Northern Ireland

McAuley 75' (og)

Parc des Princes, Paris

Attendance: 44,342 (including 7,000 Northern Ireland fans)

Referee: Martin Atkinson (England)

Michael O'Neill and first team coach Stephen Robinson chew the fat during training.

Northern Ireland returned to Paris to face the familiar faces of Wales but the ecstasy turned to agony when a heart-breaking late goal ended their Euro 2016 dream.

Michael O'Neill's men outfought, outthought and outplayed Wales for most of their last-16 showdown at the Parc des Princes but they crashed out due to a cruel Gareth McAuley own goal 15 minutes from time. McAuley, one of his country's star performers at the tournament, stretched out a leg to block Gareth Bale's exquisite cross but all he could do was poke the ball past the helpless Michael McGovern. 'This tournament has been brilliant. It's the rough with the smooth and I've been in the game long enough to understand that and keep it on an even keel. You never get too high or too low,' said McAuley.

He added, 'It's difficult now but I've enjoyed this tournament. But there are a lot of lads in there devastated. I'm gutted at the way it's ended but worse things happen in life. I'm just gutted everyone has to go home … It's been fantastic, we've embraced it and we've enjoyed it. Maybe when I look back on it in a few weeks it might help that Hal Robson-Kanu would have scored anyway but not at the minute. I'm just gutted for all the lads after all the effort they put in – but I'll take that rather than a younger lad miss a penalty in a shootout!'

The late Noel Brotherston scored the winning goal against Wales to clinch the Home International Championship in 1980 – Northern Ireland's only win over them in 40 years – and Northern Ireland deserved so much more in this encounter. O'Neill brought striker Kyle Lafferty back into the starting line-up for the first time since the first group game against Poland. Real Madrid superstar Bale couldn't get a look-in for much of the game with Stuart Dallas and Jonny Evans doubling up on him.

Going forward, it was Northern Ireland carrying the greater threat. The first real chance of the game came on 10 minutes when Stuart Dallas let fly with a low, angled strike with the outside of his left foot after evading Chris Gunter but Wayne Hennessey was equal to the task. Wales had the ball in the back of the net when Aaron Ramsey poked home after a Sam Vokes nod-down but the flag was up for offside.

Hennessey was called into action again midway through the half when he tipped a Jamie Ward effort onto

Michael O'Neill addresses the players at training on their return to Paris – and the Parc des Princes – to play Wales.

Michael McGovern plays catch-the-ball.

The Northern Ireland wall jump in unison as Gareth Bale fires a free-kick goalwards.

Welsh forward Hal Robson-Kanu wheels away in delight moments after Gareth McAuley's own goal.

Kyle Lafferty having a laugh with Aaron Hughes and Jamie Ward.

the roof of the net. The only blight on an impressive first-half display came when Dallas picked up his second booking of the tournament for the slightest of touches on Bale's toes, which meant he would miss any potential quarter final. Other than a goal, it was going perfectly to plan for O'Neill's troops.

As the second half wore on Bale and Ramsey were getting on the ball more and when they combined with 15 minutes to go it sparked misery for Northern Ireland. Ramsey slipped the ball out to Bale who had drifted wide and he produced a pinpoint cross into the six-yard box. With Robson-Kanu ready to tap it home, McAuley diverted it into his own net. It was the proverbial sucker punch from Wales, who had been on the ropes for most of the contest. Wales, of course, went on

to defeat Belgium in the last eight before bowing out of Euro 2016 at the semi-final stage when they lost to eventual winners Portugal.

Dejected manager Michael O'Neill said, 'I felt we had the better of that, to be honest. It's a very, very cruel way to lose a game and I don't think we deserved to lose it with a goal of that nature. I'm not going to point the finger at Gareth or blame him in any shape or form. He had a split-second decision to make and unfortunately it went against us. Gareth's not only had a great tournament, he's been a great player for me over the four years. He's really grown as a centre back and shown it in this tournament against the best centre forwards.' Northern Ireland had dared to dream and – despite the heartache in Paris – they lived the dream in France.

The Welsh players celebrate the goal that separated the sides in Paris.

Corry Evans
challenges
Aaron Ramsey.

NORTHERN IRELAND LINE-UP

1 Michael McGovern
18 Aaron Hughes
4 Gareth McAuley
(Josh Magennis 84')
20 Craig Cathcart
5 Jonny Evans
8 Steven Davis (c)
19 Jamie Ward
(Conor Washington 69')
13 Corry Evans
16 Oliver Norwood
(Niall McGinn 79')
14 Stuart Dallas
10 Kyle Lafferty

SUBSTITUTES

2 Conor McLaughlin
3 Shane Ferguson
6 Chris Baird
7 Niall McGinn
9 Will Grigg
11 Conor Washington
12 Roy Carroll
15 Luke McCullough
17 Paddy McNair
21 Josh Magennis
22 Lee Hodson
23 Alan Mannus

Stuart Dallas takes on Welsh defender Chris Gunter.

Steven Davis is closely watched by Neil Taylor.

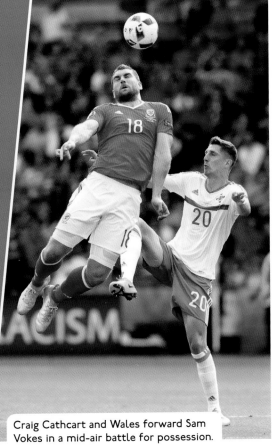
Craig Cathcart and Wales forward Sam Vokes in a mid-air battle for possession.

Northern Ireland gave it one last push as the final whistle beckoned. Here Gareth Bale prepares to head clear as Michael McGovern hopes to get on the end of a delivery into the Welsh penalty area.

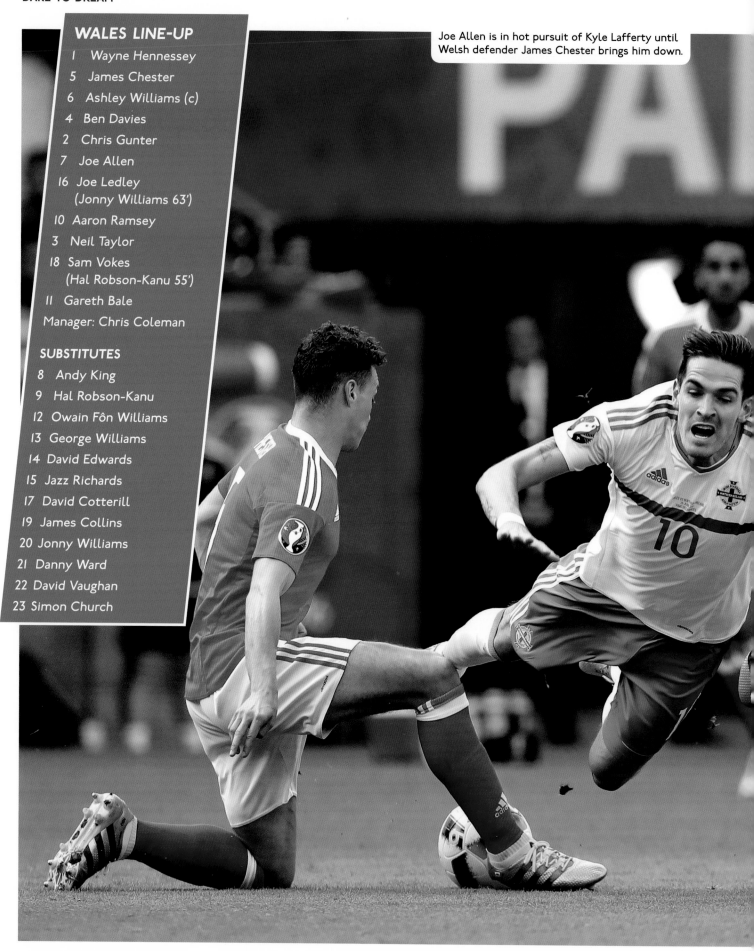

WALES LINE-UP

1   Wayne Hennessey

5   James Chester

6   Ashley Williams (c)

4   Ben Davies

2   Chris Gunter

7   Joe Allen

16   Joe Ledley
    (Jonny Williams 63')

10   Aaron Ramsey

3   Neil Taylor

18   Sam Vokes
    (Hal Robson-Kanu 55')

11   Gareth Bale

Manager: Chris Coleman

SUBSTITUTES

8   Andy King

9   Hal Robson-Kanu

12   Owain Fôn Williams

13   George Williams

14   David Edwards

15   Jazz Richards

17   David Cotterill

19   James Collins

20   Jonny Williams

21   Danny Ward

22   David Vaughan

23   Simon Church

Joe Allen is in hot pursuit of Kyle Lafferty until Welsh defender James Chester brings him down.

It's all over... Josh Magennis falls to his knees as the final whistle blows, ending Northern Ireland's magnificent run in the tournament.

James Chester consoles Aaron Hughes after the Welsh squeezed into the quarter-finals thanks to a 1-0 victory. Wales would go on to reach the semis where they lost to eventual Euro 2016 winners Portugal.

Craig Cathcart is crestfallen after Northern Ireland exit the tournament.

Fermanagh lads Michael McGovern and Kyle Lafferty embrace.

Irish FA President Jim Shaw commiserates with Steven Davis as the captain's daughters Kaia and Chloe look on.

Kyle Lafferty is close to tears as he waves to the 7,000 Northern Ireland fans who attended the game. He took off his boots and threw them to the adoring Green and White Army.

The players stayed on the Parc des Princes pitch long after the full-time whistle to applaud the Northern Ireland fans for their support and to say au revoir to Euro 2016.

Northern Ireland fans travelled in their thousands to watch their heroes in France. There were 10,000 of them in Stade de Nice for Northern Ireland's first game against Poland.

CHAPTER FIVE

THE GREEN AND WHITE ARMY

From Nice to Lyon and on to Paris, Northern Ireland supporters made sure France was awash with green and white.

Their good-natured 'craic' endeared them to the locals as well as to the many thousands of travelling fans from other nations. But while their thirst for a good time was known throughout Europe, it was in Nice, when both Northern Ireland and Poland fans were attacked during frightening scenes, that it became clear just what Northern Ireland fans are made of. That night, stories and pictures filtered through of the compassion of the Green and White Army towards the Polish fans. Next day Poland and Northern Ireland supporters were seen chatting and having a laugh together in the city-centre fanzone and travelling to the Stade de Nice together. And that kind of behaviour and attitude was typical of the Northern Ireland fans at the tournament. They happily mingled with the fans of opposing teams as well as with locals at every venue. For a brief few days they became part of the community and even managed to add a few unfamiliar faces to their already impressive numbers. But the biggest party was to come in Lyon. With the Stade de Lyon bathed in green, goals from Gareth McAuley and Niall McGinn secured Northern Ireland's first ever European Championship finals victory. Ulster actor Jimmy Nesbitt joined the celebrations that lasted long into the night. The party quickly moved to Paris where the Norn Iron bug had bitten the world champions. Die Mannschaft's fans were singing 'Will Grigg's On Fire' and they had his name on German flags. Michael O'Neill's men may have lost their final two games but the Green and White Army were the stars of the show against Germany and Wales.

Sadly, the tournament was also marked by tragedy. Just hours after watching Northern Ireland's opening game against Poland in Nice, Darren Rodgers (24) from Ballymena died following a fall. Rivalries were put to one side as Republic of Ireland fans sang 'Stand Up For The Ulstermen' in the 24th minute of their clash

The Green and White Army wore a colourful array of glasses in France.

Lots of fans painted their faces and donned costumes to support the boys in green.

Now that's how to wear a beret!

A lot of time and effort went in to creating this headgear.

with Sweden. Days later, at the Ukraine match in Lyon, 16,000 members of the Green and White Army remembered one of their own in the 24th minute when a banner was unfurled and Ukraine fans joined their counterparts in paying tribute. But no one could have envisaged that further tragedy was to follow. Belfast man Robert Rainey (64) took ill during the first half of the Ukraine match and, despite desperate efforts by medics to revive him following his collapse, he sadly died in the stand while the game was taking place. Michael O'Neill, his players and the Irish FA joined fans in honouring both supporters and the team wore black armbands in memory of two fans who went to France to follow their heroes and didn't come home.

At home, Euro 2016 fever swept our wee country. There were many people who had never previously even watched a Northern Ireland match on television who made sure they were at the fanzones set up in each county. Games were shown on giant screens in towns up and down the country, from Lisburn to Cookstown and from Newtownabbey to Bangor, while tens of thousands descended on the fanzone at the Belsonic concert site beside Titanic Belfast. Before the tournament, manager Michael O'Neill said, 'The support during qualification was incredible and a big part of us getting to the finals in the first place. We're grateful so many are making the trip to France, but anyone watching the games back in Northern Ireland has a crucial role to play as well. The idea of thousands of Northern Ireland fans gathering at the Euros Fanzone at Titanic back in Belfast will be another huge motivation for the players.' Videos of the fans at home singing and dancing throughout the tournament were replayed all over the world and the Green and White Army became almost as big a draw as the team's exploits in France. The central fanzone in Belfast moved to Boucher Playing Fields ahead of the last-16 clash with Wales, due to Belsonic using the grounds at Titanic for a gig, but once again the fans came out in their droves to show their support for the team.

115

The Northern Ireland fans were in full voice at all the games.

Northern Ireland supporters go for a dip in the
Mediterranean before the game against Poland in Nice.

Come on Northern Ireland!

A young fan shows his support in the
huge fan zone close to the Eiffel Tower
in Paris before the game against Germany.

Fans of all ages attended the matches in
France, including this tiny tot who was at
the Germany game in Parc des Princes.

The beard says it all!

Several of the shops in Saint-Georges-de-Reneins had window displays welcoming the Northern Ireland team to their area. This one was a perfect backdrop for a couple of fans who tried to play baguettes!

Rocking out in the stands with the aid of plastic geetars.

Cool FM's breakfast team – Rebecca McKinney, Paulo Ross, Pete Snodden and reporter Alex Keery – broadcast from France every morning. They also enjoyed the games!

So who was the mystery man behind this MA-NI-AC outfit?

Northern Ireland fans greet Super Victor, the mascot for the Euro 2016 tournament in France.

Anxious faces in the crowd at the Round of 16 game against Wales in Paris.

Another beret enthusiastic fan.

The feather is a nice touch ...

The stadiums became Party Central for thousands of fans.

Members of the Green and White Army fully colour co-ordinated.

The beard and beret combo was very popular.

Many fans brought a wee taste of home with them.

The fanzone at Titanic Belfast, the venue for the homecoming event for the team, attracted more than 40,000 people during the group games, while a further fanzone at Boucher Playing Fields – run by Belfast City Council for the Round of 16 game against Wales – attracted around 9,000 fans.

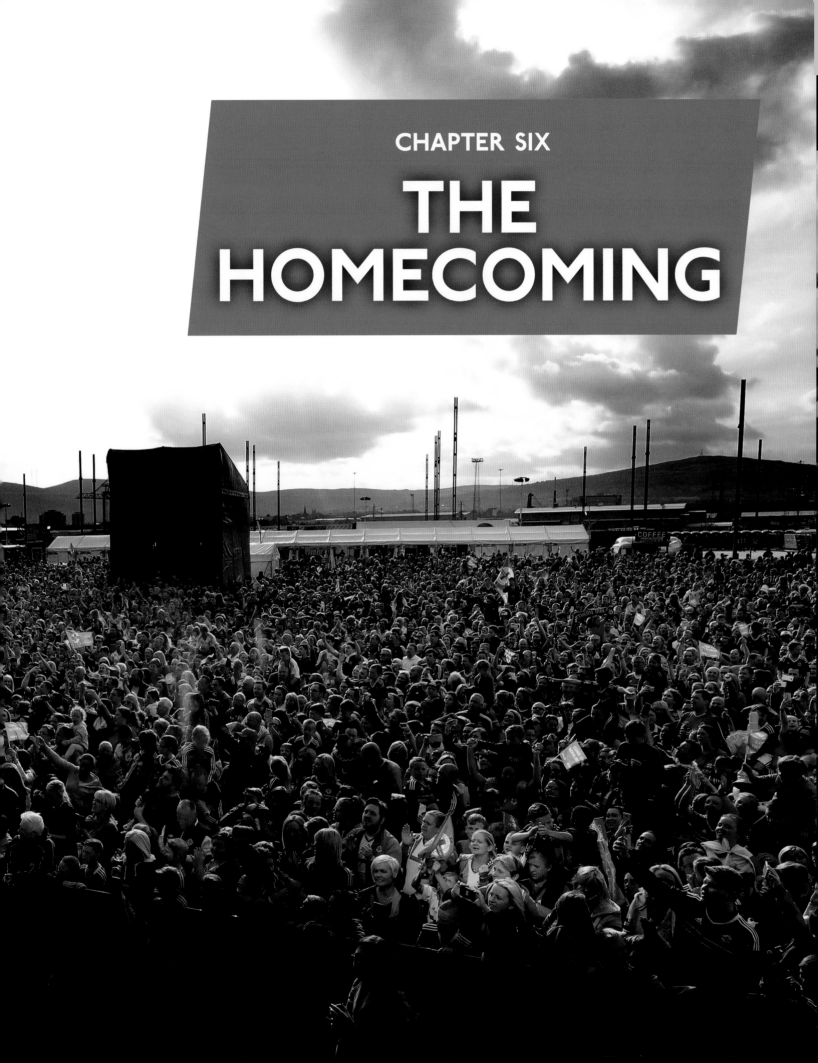

CHAPTER SIX

THE HOMECOMING

Northern Ireland's Euro 2016 heroes felt more like rock stars or members of One Direction when they arrived home from France.

An interactive social media wall had given the players and staff a flavour of what the public back home thought about their achievements but nothing prepared them for the unbridled exuberance, jubilation and irresistible good humour of the homecoming event at the fanzone beside Titanic Belfast.

It seemed to take ages for the squad to appear on the stage, but nobody minded. 'To the best fans in the world,' said the huge screen above the Belsonic stage. 'You made all the difference. Thank you.' Memories of the tournament were fresh but they would last a lifetime for the players and fans. Footage of all four games was played, as were moments like the Northern Ireland fans singing 'Happy Birthday' to a German supporter and the Northern Ireland and Wales fans reuniting a lost young supporter with his dad in Paris. And as if that wasn't enough there was even Eric Cantona performing a very Gallic version of 'Will Grigg's On Fire' on the screen. But the fans were there for one reason: to see their heroes. Standing in the evening sunshine, with the great shipyard cranes in the background, singing and selfies were the order of the day as fans acknowledged the terrific achievements of the players who in turn got to thank the Green and White Army for their incredible support.

Staff at Belfast International Airport formed a guard of honour to welcome the players home. They returned to Northern Ireland via a charter flight from Lyon.

Fans take pictures of the team bus as it makes its way from the airport to the fanzone at Titanic Belfast where nearly 10,000 fans were waiting to greet the players.

Northern Ireland First Minister Arlene Foster, who attended a couple of Northern Ireland's games in France, met Michael O'Neill and the players behind the scenes at the homecoming event, which was arranged by the Department for Communities and run by Navigator Blue.

The homecoming event was shown live on television by BBC Northern Ireland and sports presenter Stephen Watson, who covered the tourney in France, acted as MC. Here he chats to Michael McGovern about his Euro 2016 experience.

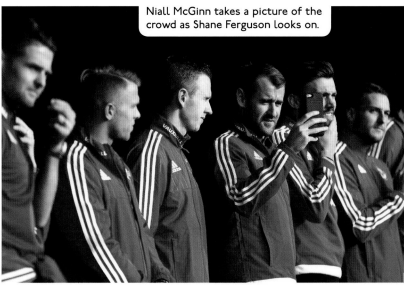

Niall McGinn takes a picture of the crowd as Shane Ferguson looks on.

The squad and the backroom staff on stage.

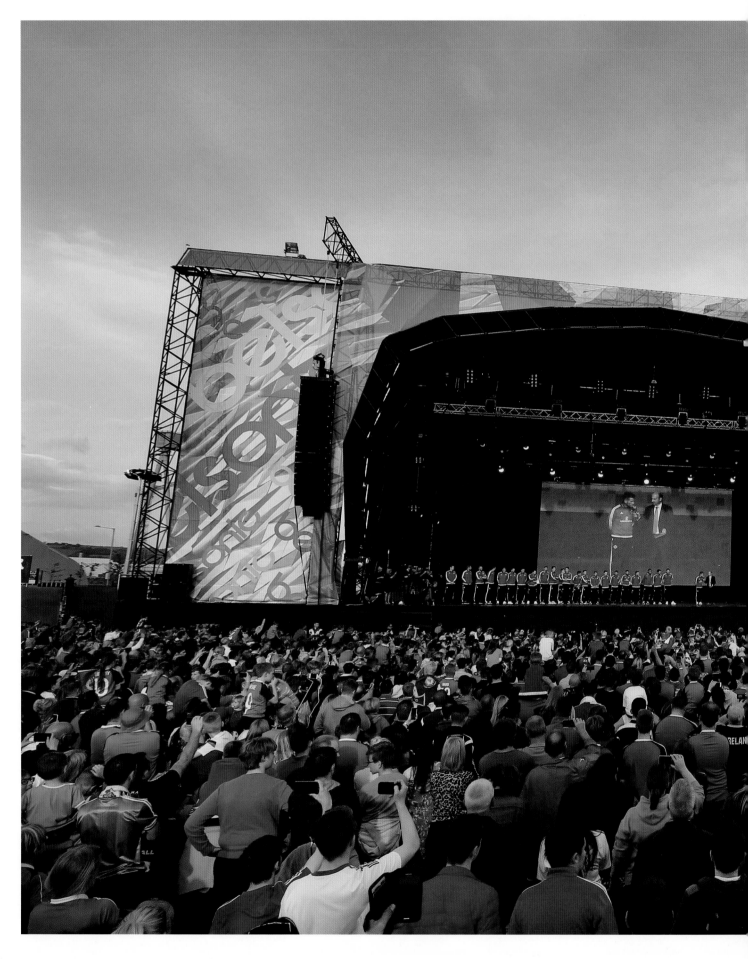

The fans created an electric atmosphere at the homecoming event.

Fans young and old flocked to the Belfast event.

Gareth McAuley is applauded by fellow defenders Jonny Evans and Craig Cathcart.

The setting and the weather played their part in making the homecoming event extra special.

The fans watch spellbound.

Michael O'Neill is interviewed by Stephen Watson.

Niall McGinn and Gareth McAuley, Northern Ireland's scorers at Euro 2016, are all smiles at the homecoming event.

The squad and backroom staff are clearly on cloud nine.

Ballymena boys together ... Michael O'Neill and senior kitman Raymond Millar (fourth from right).

Josh Magennis takes a selfie as the players dance a merry jig.

Stunning backdrop ... Gareth McAuley and Josh Magennis put themselves and the crowd in the frame at the homecoming event.

The squad give Michael O'Neill the bumps.

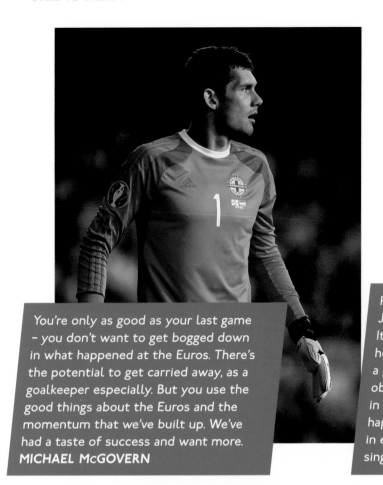

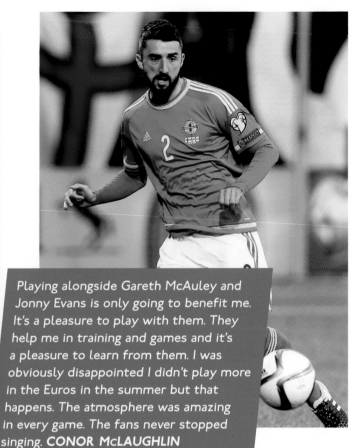

You're only as good as your last game – you don't want to get bogged down in what happened at the Euros. There's the potential to get carried away, as a goalkeeper especially. But you use the good things about the Euros and the momentum that we've built up. We've had a taste of success and want more.
MICHAEL McGOVERN

Playing alongside Gareth McAuley and Jonny Evans is only going to benefit me. It's a pleasure to play with them. They help me in training and games and it's a pleasure to learn from them. I was obviously disappointed I didn't play more in the Euros in the summer but that happens. The atmosphere was amazing in every game. The fans never stopped singing. **CONOR McLAUGHLIN**

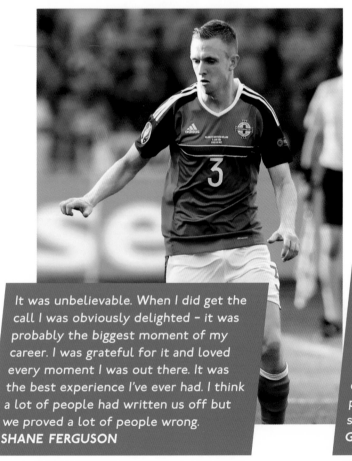

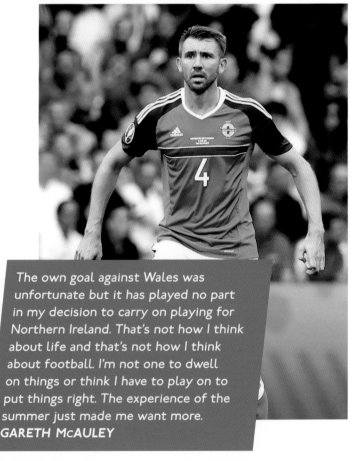

It was unbelievable. When I did get the call I was obviously delighted – it was probably the biggest moment of my career. I was grateful for it and loved every moment I was out there. It was the best experience I've ever had. I think a lot of people had written us off but we proved a lot of people wrong.
SHANE FERGUSON

The own goal against Wales was unfortunate but it has played no part in my decision to carry on playing for Northern Ireland. That's not how I think about life and that's not how I think about football. I'm not one to dwell on things or think I have to play on to put things right. The experience of the summer just made me want more.
GARETH McAULEY

Coming home to Belfast was fantastic. It really was an unbelievable experience. The base camp in France was excellent and I must admit after a couple of days back home I started to get withdrawal symptoms. After the Euros people were coming up to me in the street, congratulating us all for making the country proud, and that is something I'd never experienced. **JONNY EVANS**

Qualification for Euro 2016 was the icing on the cake for my international career before retiring. I have lined out with some great players over the past 13 years and I would like to thank the managers, coaches and Irish FA staff that I have worked with over that time. I would also like to thank the Northern Ireland fans who have been absolutely tremendous. **CHRIS BAIRD**

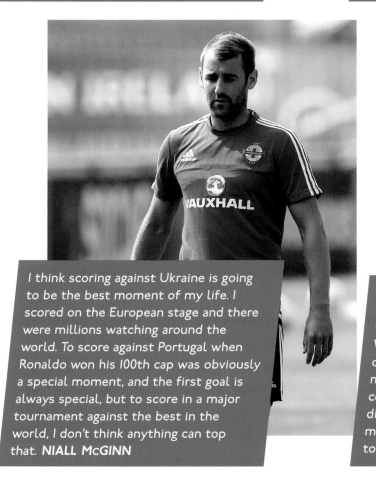

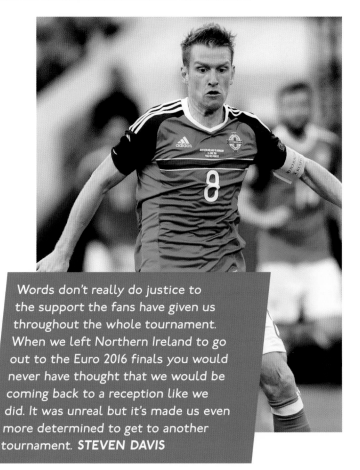

I think scoring against Ukraine is going to be the best moment of my life. I scored on the European stage and there were millions watching around the world. To score against Portugal when Ronaldo won his 100th cap was obviously a special moment, and the first goal is always special, but to score in a major tournament against the best in the world, I don't think anything can top that. **NIALL McGINN**

Words don't really do justice to the support the fans have given us throughout the whole tournament. When we left Northern Ireland to go out to the Euro 2016 finals you would never have thought that we would be coming back to a reception like we did. It was unreal but it's made us even more determined to get to another tournament. **STEVEN DAVIS**

It was unbelievable. It was brilliant to hear the song at Wigan but to then hear it on a huge scale at the Euros was something else. Our fans have been unbelievable – I think there's a special feeling between the players and the fans. The song is one thing, but to come to a tournament like the Euros and not play, as a professional footballer, was massively disappointing. **WILL GRIGG**

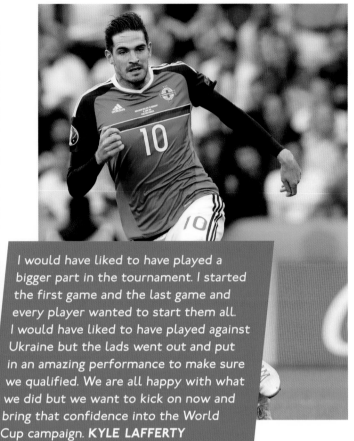

I would have liked to have played a bigger part in the tournament. I started the first game and the last game and every player wanted to start them all. I would have liked to have played against Ukraine but the lads went out and put in an amazing performance to make sure we qualified. We are all happy with what we did but we want to kick on now and bring that confidence into the World Cup campaign. **KYLE LAFFERTY**

It's devastating when the final whistle goes and you realise you're out. It was an unbelievable journey and none of us wanted it to end. It's such a harsh way to go out as well. We were devastated to go out at that point but we gave everything and I don't think we can have any regrets looking back. **CONOR WASHINGTON**

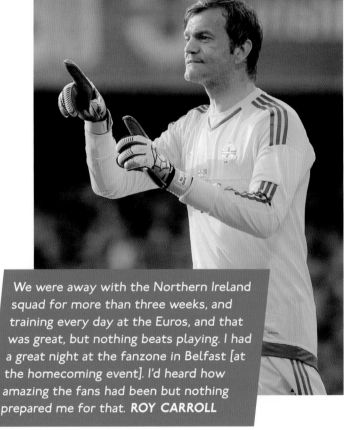

We were away with the Northern Ireland squad for more than three weeks, and training every day at the Euros, and that was great, but nothing beats playing. I had a great night at the fanzone in Belfast [at the homecoming event]. I'd heard how amazing the fans had been but nothing prepared me for that. **ROY CARROLL**

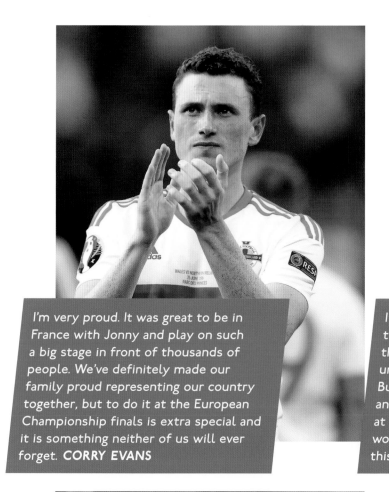

I'm very proud. It was great to be in France with Jonny and play on such a big stage in front of thousands of people. We've definitely made our family proud representing our country together, but to do it at the European Championship finals is extra special and it is something neither of us will ever forget. **CORRY EVANS**

I think we've done everyone proud and the fans have done us proud. They are the best fans in the world and it was just unfortunate that we couldn't go further. But it was an unbelievable experience and we believe we deserve to be playing at that level now but we have to be working hard and improving to make sure this is just the start. **STUART DALLAS**

I wanted to make Michael's mind up that I was good enough to warrant a place in the squad. I would have gone to France as a fan if I hadn't been selected but going as part of the squad was very special to me. In our downtime I was king of table tennis while Niall McGinn was king of the pool table. **LUKE McCULLOUGH**

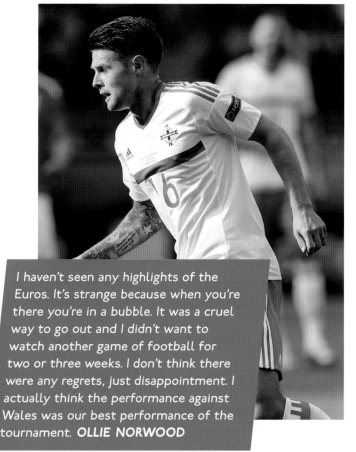

I haven't seen any highlights of the Euros. It's strange because when you're there you're in a bubble. It was a cruel way to go out and I didn't want to watch another game of football for two or three weeks. I don't think there were any regrets, just disappointment. I actually think the performance against Wales was our best performance of the tournament. **OLLIE NORWOOD**

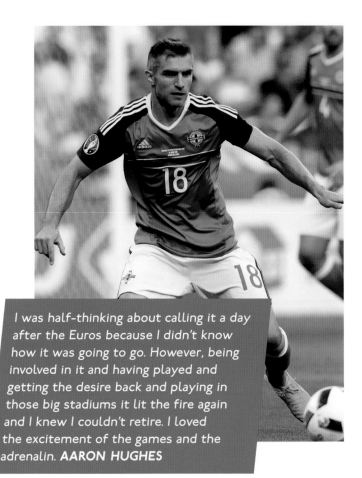

I went away to the Euros and that was a fantastic experience, one I will never forget, but I knew I wanted first team football this season. I played 24 times for Manchester United in the past two seasons but knew I needed to move. My career has really taken off and I don't want to look back. **PADDY McNAIR**

I was half-thinking about calling it a day after the Euros because I didn't know how it was going to go. However, being involved in it and having played and getting the desire back and playing in those big stadiums it lit the fire again and I knew I couldn't retire. I loved the excitement of the games and the adrenalin. **AARON HUGHES**

Pundits said we wouldn't score a goal and we wouldn't win a game. It's great to shut them up and prove people wrong. Now going into the World Cup campaign we'll do the whole country proud again. We've always been written off and called the underdogs. We were still called the underdogs when we won the group in qualifying for France. **JAMIE WARD**

It was an amazing experience seeing all our fans in France and hearing what was going on back home. When we went out into each stadium to take a look at the pitch, the fans were already singing even then. It was an incredible experience, not just to play at a major tournament but to experience everything it had to offer. **CRAIG CATHCART**

Euro 2016 raised our profile. If you can do something that grabs somebody's attention it always bodes well for you and it helped get my move. I have learnt a lot from the tournament. Six weeks with 22 other players is a long time and the majority of those players are in the Premier League and Championship so the standard of their training is very high.
JOSH MAGENNIS

It was a great experience being at the Euros and the icing on the cake was signing for Rangers afterwards. As a kid you always wish to go to a major tournament or be part of it. Obviously I would like to have got some minutes and a bit of game time out there, but experiencing the whole tournament was a massive learning curve for me.
LEE HODSON

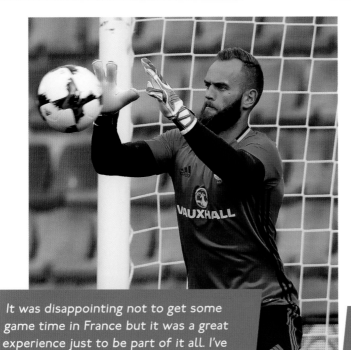

It was disappointing not to get some game time in France but it was a great experience just to be part of it all. I've watched Euros and World Cups on TV in the past and I never thought I'd see anything like it with a Northern Ireland squad. Everything about the organisation was first class. The facilities couldn't have been better. **ALAN MANNUS**

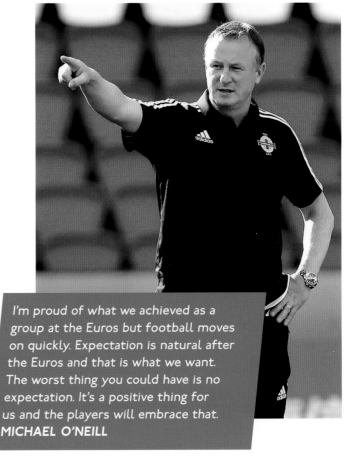

I'm proud of what we achieved as a group at the Euros but football moves on quickly. Expectation is natural after the Euros and that is what we want. The worst thing you could have is no expectation. It's a positive thing for us and the players will embrace that.
MICHAEL O'NEILL

THE MEDAL OF THE CITY OF PARIS

The Green and White Army made a lasting impression on Euro 2016, adding colour and an unforgettable atmosphere to the tournament.

The fans, who travelled to France in their thousands, were talked about long after they returned home in June. Their contribution to the competition was marked not only by UEFA but also by the awarding of the Grand Vermeil – the Medal of the City of Paris – which is the most prestigious honour and is awarded to cultural and political figures.

'They participated in the festive atmosphere that has been prevailing in Paris these last two weeks,' said Jean-François Martins, Deputy Mayor for sport and tourism. 'They are a model for all the supporters of the world. As shown in the numerous videos that circulate on the social networks, the Parisians particularly appreciated meeting them, speaking with them and sharing those joyful moments that are essential in such a great sportive event.' The Executive Committee of UEFA reviewed the tournament and decided to give an award to the Irish FA as well as to the football

associations of Iceland, Republic of Ireland and Wales for their fans' outstanding contributions to Euro 2016. UEFA President Aleksander Čeferin said: 'UEFA Euro 2016 was a celebration of football and this is thanks in large part to the passion and dedication of fans at all stadiums in France. UEFA wanted to reward some of the groups of supporters that were particularly enthusiastic and passionate during the tournament so congratulations to the national associations who are receiving this award.'

The medal presented to Northern Ireland fans by the Mayor of Paris, Madame Anne Hidalgo, as a mark of gratitude for their exemplary behaviour in the city during Euro 2016.

CANCER FUND FOR CHILDREN

THE OFFICIAL CHARITY OF THE NORTHERN IRELAND TEAM

The players were keen to give something back to Northern Ireland long before a ball was kicked at Euro 2016.

Cancer Fund for Children was chosen as the official charity and the squad supported its work through various initiatives, including donating match fees as well as the selling of limited-edition ties from the Irish FA's official menswear provider, Bogart. The charity, which supports children who are living with cancer, was never far from the minds of the travelling party in France and they were delighted to receive special messages from some of the children staying in the charity's Daisy Lodge complex who had made 'Good Luck' posters for the players.

Supporters also played their part and £10,800 was raised through onsite collections during the televised games at the fanzone at Titanic Belfast as well through ticket sales for the homecoming event. Irish FA President David Martin, who took over the role from Jim Shaw as Northern Ireland's Euro adventure drew to a close, said: 'It is great that the event has benefited the Cancer Fund for Children. The members of the squad were all keen to give something back to the community.' Sorcha Mac Laimhin from Cancer Fund for Children added: 'Cancer Fund for Children are delighted to have been working with the Northern Ireland football team and the Irish FA during the Euros and we really appreciate the support the Green and White Army gave us.'

Michael McGovern and Gareth McAuley read messages of support for the team from children who are supported by Cancer Fund for Children.

The win over Greece in Belfast in September 2015 saw us book our place at Euro 2016.

ACKNOWLEDGEMENTS

ABOUT THE AUTHORS

WILLIAM CHERRY is a senior photographer with Press Eye, a Belfast-based photo agency. He has been covering Northern Ireland games for more than 25 years. His first away trip was in 1994 and he has travelled extensively with the team since then. Press Eye are the Irish FA's official photographers.

Additional pictures for this book were supplied by Press Eye photographers Kelvin Boyes, Matt Mackey, Jonathan Porter, Brian Little, Kevin Scott and Stephen Hamilton.

MARK McINTOSH is the football writer in Northern Ireland for *The Sun*. He has covered the international team at home and abroad for the last 17 years. He was the only print journalist to cover all of Northern Ireland's Euro 2016 qualifiers and the four games in France.

NIGEL TILSON is a senior media officer with the Irish Football Association. He worked as a journalist for 25 years and is a former newspaper editor, business editor and sports editor. He has held senior roles in public relations and public affairs since 2008.

Irish Football Association

Official publication by Irish Football Association
National Football Stadium at Windsor Park,
Donegall Avenue, Belfast, BT12 6LW

President
David Martin

Deputy Presidents
Jack Grundie and Crawford Wilson

Chief Executive
Patrick Nelson

Pictures
Press Eye

Editor
Nigel Tilson

Head of Communications
Neil Brittain

Published in association with
Blackstaff Press
4D Weavers Court, Linfield Road,
Belfast, BT12 5GH